THE
AMERICAN
PEOPLE

THE
AMERICAN
PEOPLE

A STUDY IN
NATIONAL
CHARACTER

BY *GEOFFREY GORER*

REVISED EDITION

NEW YORK

W · W · NORTON & COMPANY · INC ·

Library of Congress Catalog Card No. 64-11138

SBN 393 00262 4

PRINTED IN THE UNITED STATES OF AMERICA

5 6 7 8 9

TO THE MEMORY OF

ERLING C. OLSEN, JR.,
half Norwegian, half Czech, good American
killed in Normandy, July, 1944

AND

JOHN SALT,
North American Director of the BBC during
the war, who was the first to suggest that
this book be written. He died unexpectedly
in Manchester, England, December, 1947.

CONTENTS

FOREWORD—1963

THE BODY of this book remains as I wrote it in 1947 and 1948. To the extent that the generalizations were valid then, they are still valid. Minor changes, such as the increased importance of television and the greatly decreased importance of radio, will be obvious to every reader.

In a few cases I have wished to modify what I had written previously, or to add a more recent illustration; these places are indicated by a footnote designated by a letter of the alphabet such as [a]; the notes will in all cases be found at the end of the relevant chapter.

I have added a postscript "Foreign Matter" to touch on the themes which, in the first months of 1963, seemed to me new developments since this book was written.

Sunte House,   Geoffrey Gorer
Haywards Heath,
Sussex.

May 1963

FOREWORD

Underneath all, individuals,
I swear nothing is good to me now that ignores individuals,
The American compact is altogether with individuals,
The only government is that which makes minute with in-
    dividuals . . .

           Walt Whitman, *By Blue Ontario's Shore*

IN THIS book I am trying to apply some of the methods and insights of cultural anthropology to a great modern community. I first visited the United States in 1935, and received there my training in anthropology from Drs. Mead, Benedict, and Dollard; and since that date a series of accidents has kept the two themes dominant in my life. In 1936–37 I made a field trip—as I then thought, the first of several—among the Lepchas of Sikkim; but I came back with my health permanently impaired so that, at least for several years, I could not contemplate another expedition among primitives, with the inevitable discomfort, bad food, and separation from doctors.

I was therefore very glad to accept an invitation from the Rockefeller Foundation to make a study on the impact of films and radio on American audiences from an "anthropological point of view." Although this study was inevitably only a preliminary survey of a very wide field, it had, for me, the advantage of taking me over much of the United States and acquainting me with the work of American sociologists in these and allied fields. When this survey was completed I was invited by the director, Dr. Mark May, to join the staff of the Institute of Human Relations of Yale University. Besides the opportunities which this invitation gave me to improve my understanding and knowledge of anthropology, behavorist psychology, and psychoanalysis, it also provided the occasion for a detailed study of American childhood and youth. A psychoanalyst on the staff of the Institute, Mr. Earl Zinn, had analyzed over four years a young New Englander who had developed schizophrenia, and had had electrically recorded the whole of this analysis. Mr. Zinn asked me to collaborate in preparing the life history of this young man from the enormous amount of material so recorded. Since I lacked any standard to determine what was "normal" in the subject's childhood and schooldays, I had to investigate the established patterns by interviewing and some survey work. To discover what was peculiar in the early life and behavior of this young schizophrenic I had to study fairly consistently the early lives of Americans who did not develop such symptoms. Much of the material in this book, particularly that on childhood and youth, is derived from these researches.

From Yale I went to Washington, D. C., to join one of the British wartime missions. Part of the work which I then had to do was to act as liaison, to represent the

London office in meetings with representatives of its American counterparts, and to report back to London American attitudes, criticisms, and suggestions. Despite the excellent collaboration which generally existed in a shared effort to a common goal, this work threw into high relief the basic themes of disagreement and disapproval which, even though muted under the stress of war, were present in the minds of most of my British and American colleagues. Owing to the fact that many of my American "opposite numbers" were former professional colleagues, I heard a lot of frank criticism of British activities which politeness kept hidden in formal meetings.

After experiences extending over several years it is clear to me that, infinitely varied as are the occasions for Anglo-American disagreements, there is a single basic attitude underlying the vast majority. The English become disapproving, contemptuous or angry because the Americans do not act or think or talk as the English would do in their place; the Americans become disapproving, contemptuous or angry because the English do not act or think or talk as the Americans would do in their place. Because English and Americans share variants of the same language, the same religions, the same political ideas, the same laws, and the same physical types, each group expects the other to be a near replica of itself, and is continually being disillusioned and distressed when this expectation is proved to be unjustified.

Although the existence of these shared elements has considerable bearing on the long-term political relations between the two countries, I am convinced that, on the day-to-day level, this belief in the identity or similarity of the English and Americans is the greatest stumbling block that exists to mutual understanding and collaboration between the two peoples.

Two hundred years ago the similarities between the inhabitants of England and those of the American colonies were almost certainly far greater than their differences. But the differing experiences and development of the last two centuries have resulted in the two societies evolving strongly contrasting systems of values, typical ways of behaving, views of the universe, and pictures which each holds of itself in the world—in a word, most strongly contrasting national characters.

These differences are fundamental. There is no question of one way of behaving being better, the other worse, one character more praiseworthy and one more blamable; there is no proper occasion for invidious comparisons. Only the most limited and provincial people would consider that the Chinese were "wrong" or "immoral" to dress in white for mourning because we show our sorrow with black clothes; both devices accomplish effectively the same social ends. Similarly, we admit that different groups of people have varied preferences concerning the food with which they relieve their hunger, without becoming morally indignant over the fact. We might dislike it if attempts were made to force us to eat the foods which other societies prefer; but who considers it "wrong" or "immoral" for the Chinese to enjoy bird's nests, or the Eskimo rotten seal meat, or the Australian aborigines wichity grubs? And who among us considers it reasonable of the

Moslems to damn us for eating pork, or of the Hindus to despise us for eating beef? But when it is a question of values, of different ways of looking at and interpreting the world, of different emphases and reticences, of different hopes and fears, our judicial impartiality is likely to leave us. Our ways, we feel and proclaim, are the only right ways; all others are wrong and approximate to rightness only as they approximate to ours; we seek to impose a single standard, and become distressed and angry when other peoples seem not even to recognize those truths which we hold to be self-evident.

It is this inevitable ethnocentrism which makes the discussion of the national character of equals and contemporaries so difficult and so delicate. A statement whose intention is purely objective is liable to be interpreted as criticism by readers of any nationality. If the reader is of the nationality being discussed he is likely to interpret the objective tone as though it were a denial of appreciation and love, a feeling in some ways analogous to that evoked by hearing a recording of one's own voice; if he be of another nationality there is a strong temptation to make self-satisfied judgments about the differences between the behavior described and his own partial and complacent view of his own character and society: "Thank God I am not as other men are . . ."

To minimize as much as might be both the feeling of unfriendly criticism and the Pharisaical self-satisfaction, I have avoided as far as possible making comparisons between American behavior and that of any other society, and also the pointing out of similarities. In particular, I

have avoided any references to comparable English
behavior, except in the very few occasions when it seemed
necessary to develop the different significances given to the
same words. I am aware that there are some sections which
might as well be describing English as American behavior;
but drawing attention to these points would only appear
meaningful if comparisons were developed systematically
on all points.

The desire to avoid evoking feelings of unfriendly
criticism or of Pharisaical self-satisfaction has been one of
the motives for eschewing comparisons; an even more
compelling reason is my ignorance. I do not know enough
about England [a] (or any European society) to make consistent comparisons. Apart from the astigmatism which we
all invariably have for our own society and its values, I am
limited and biased by my own education and class; I have
not had opportunities for studying English life in any way
comparable to those I have had for studying that of the
Americans; my range of social contacts has been far less;
even geographically I know far less of England than I do of
the United States. Except for the briefest visits I know
only southern and central England; I don't think that in
the whole of my life I have spent two months north of
Cambridge. In America I have been in over forty of the
forty-eight states; there are only two regions which I do
not know at all—the Southwest (New Mexico, Arizona,
Nevada) and the Northwest (Washington, Oregon,
Idaho); although these are of great geographical extent
they are very sparsely populated, the six states containing
only about 3 per cent of the total population, and I do not

think that this ignorance seriously vitiates any of the conclusions drawn. The greater part of my time in the United States was spent in Washington, D. C.; although this curious city, whose one industry is government, is probably not in itself representative of anything outside its own exiguous district borders, it does bring together in its small compass many inhabitants of every state in the Union.

This book is concerned with only about two thirds of the inhabitants of the United States. The history, the traditions, and even to a large extent the population of the southern states and to a lesser degree Texas, rural New England, and California contrast so strongly with those of the remaining portion of the country that proper consideration would demand for each of these subcultures treatment nearly as extensive as this book. With the exception of Chapter Eight I am not considering the more obvious minorities, whether ethnic, religious, or social, inside this restricted area. It is also perhaps necessary to emphasize that I am only describing the people of the United States during the last ten years.

Even though the most striking exceptions are excluded, it would appear difficult to make valid generalizations about nearly a hundred million people scattered over half a continent. In the old world this objection would have more strength; centuries of isolation, of local traditions, of inbreeding could be expected to produce profound differences between different groups and different localities. But, with few exceptions, American history lacks precisely this isolation, these local traditions, this inbreeding. Away from the Atlantic coast, the bulk of America's population arrived but little ahead of the railways; few had such strong attachment to a given locality that generations passed their life in the same place; and local traditions cannot root very deep on soil which, little more than a century ago, was roamed by Indians and buffaloes. There is of course noticeable variation in different areas; in some the predominance of immigrants of a single tradition—for example, the Scandinavians in Minnesota, the Germans in much of Wisconsin, Illinois, and Pennsylvania, the Irish in Massachusetts, the Mexicans in Texas, the French-speaking Acadians in western Louisiana—provides a local coloring; in others, the concentration of most of the population in a single pursuit—for example, mining in much of Montana or cattle raising in Wyoming—reduces the contrasts and limits the aspirations of the inhabitants; but these are only surface modifications of a common pattern.

Refined phonemic analysis of the minuter variations of speech habits can be used by an expert to discover within a hundred miles where a given American was raised; but for two thirds of the population and three fifths of the area this is the only sure indication of local origin and upbringing. In the words of Walt Whitman, who foresaw so clearly much of the psychological development of modern America, there is the "democratic average and basic equality" which make wide generalizations possible.

It is perhaps necessary to emphasize that this concept of national character in no way denies the variations of individual personality; nor does it imply that all Americans exhibit all the characteristics hereinafter described. All that is claimed is that the concatenation of characteristics and patterns of behavior ascribed to the group are exhibited by a significant number of the members of that group, and are approved of, or are assented to, by most of the remainder; and that this concatenation of characteristics, these patterns of behavior, have been the most influential in molding the institutions in which the whole society lives. So, if the reader pleases, he will, each time I use the term "Americans" without qualification, expand it to read "a significant number of Americans" or "more Americans than not" or "compared with other groups, Americans are more prone to . . ."—phrases which, if used as often as meticulous accuracy would require, would make for clumsy writing and painful reading.

I have tried to isolate the consistent themes underlying and informing American actions by examining the usual and expected behavior in a number of typical relationships: child to father, child to mother, parents to children, husband and wife, lovers, friends, neighbors, business associates and rivals, employers and employees, majority to minorities, Americans to foreigners, and so on. In its extension and consistency this approach is technically a novel one. There is one major omission: the role of religion and the relationship of parishioner to clergyman are quite neglected. This omission is a serious one; particularly in the country, the social importance of Protestantism is great, and the ideas derived from it have considerable influence. This omission is due to ignorance on my part; I do not have sufficient experience or knowledge to make valid generalizations. Although I have tried consistently to think scientifically about the material available to me, exactly as I should about any other anthropological material, I did not gather my data with the deliberation I should have employed if I had planned to write this book when I was in America. Save for the study of the schizophrenic, who was a pious Congregationalist, my different employments in the United States did not bring me into consistent contact with the religious life of the country; and since my knowledge of such psychologically important events as religious revivals is entirely second or third-hand, I have preferred to omit all reference to them.

This book is the second study of the American character from what may be called the "psychocultural" point of view. In 1942 Margaret Mead wrote *And Keep Your Powder Dry* [1] to "discuss what are the strengths and weaknesses of the American character—the psychological equipment with which we can win the war." The book was primarily an attempt "with such knowledge and insights as we have to do what we can as anthropologists to win the war." With this overriding purpose in mind, Dr. Mead concentrated above all on a detailed analysis of American ethics and, except for a few glancing references, ignored those areas of American life where these ethical principles did not operate.[2] This statement of the Ameri-

[1] New York, Morrow, 1942. The two quotations are taken from Chapters II and I respectively. See also Margaret Mead's later articles on these and similar subjects which are listed in the bibliography of her article *The Application of Anthropological Technique to Cross-National Communication* (Transactions New York Academy of Sciences Vol. IX No. 4, February, 1947).

[2] Thus the only reference to business that I can find occurs in the following sentences from Chapter XI: "That there are already many

can ethical position seems to me detailed and complete, and I therefore have not tried to elaborate it. I have made a few condensed statements of Dr. Mead's conclusions and given references to the relevant chapters in her book.

In the study of the particular development of the American family, Dr. Mead's book blazed the trail which I am following. Inevitably there has been a certain amount of duplication; on those points where Dr. Mead has given full documentation I have contented myself with a summary of her conclusions. I have not entered into any controversies; interested specialists can easily discover by comparison the few occasions on which I differ from her in interpretation, and the rather more numerous ones where I differ in emphasis.

It is impossible for me to state adequately my intellectual debt to Dr. Mead. I owe to her much of my original training and orientation in cultural anthropology, the information on American character derived from her book, and many further insights on points of contrast between English and American character developed in long conversations over many years. Unfortunately I have never developed the habit of keeping notes on conversations; and it is very possible that I may have quoted without due acknowledgment ideas and formulations originally made by her. I ask pardon for such unintentional discourtesies.

I have tried not to overburden this book with a plethora

---

such Americans it is impossible to deny, just as it is impossible to ignore those scattered areas in American life in which all ideals have been sacrificed to a limbo of cynical grabbing—politics being the most notable example; business ethics often another. In whole areas of life, Americans have ceased to see any element of moral responsibility. . . ."

of footnotes, and for that reason have not drawn attention to the many cases where I have either agreed with or contradicted statements by previous writers on the same subject. I have gained insight from a number of books, among which I should like to single out Dennis Brogan's *American Problem* (London, 1943), Harold D. Lasswell's *Personal Insecurity and World Politics* (New York, 1935), Hermann Keyserling's *America Set Free* (New York, 1929), and Alexis de Tocqueville's *American Democracy* (Paris, 1834). I was not able to obtain copies of Graham Hutton's *Midwest at Noon* (Chicago, 1946) or John Gunther's *Inside U. S. A.* (New York, 1947) until I had finished this book.

I have gained a great deal of information from a systematic survey of the admirable public-opinion polls carried out by Mr. Elmo Roper for *Fortune* over the last ten years. I have not wanted to fill the text with statistical tables and therefore have made few quotations directly from this source; but a great number of the statements in this book could be given statistical verification by reference to these *Fortune* polls.

Much of the material which follows is based on talks and discussions held over many years in different parts of the United States. Since neither I nor the people I talked with were then aware that I intended writing this book, it does not seem fair to ascribe statements or views to named individuals when they have not put them in writing; but I am conscious of having derived information from Wystan Auden, Gregory Bateson, Ruth Benedict, George and Poca Dession, John and Victorine Dollard, Erik Homburger Erikson, Helen Fuller, Kay Halle, David Hearfield IV, Allen Holmberg, Irving and Marjorie Janis, Isa Jennings, Lincoln Kirstein, Ernst and Marianne Kris, Harold Lasswell, Nathan Leites, Paul and Margaret Linebarger, John and Mary Marshall, Mark and Ruby May, Alfred and Rhoda Metraux, Pete and Carmen Murdock, Philleo and Edith Nash, Cornelius and Harriet Osgood, Nelson and Henrietta Poynter, Jack Roberts, Leo and Priscilla Rosten, John and Olive Salt, David Schneider, Hans Speier, Elinor Stuart, George and Roberta Taylor, Mary Taylor, John and Beatrice Whiting, and Earl Zinn. I hope they will all accept my grateful thanks. I should also like to thank the librarians of the American Library of Information in London for their courteous assistance.

I owe a very special debt of gratitude to Professor Edward Shils of the University of London and of the University of Chicago. He read an early draft of this book with great care and made many criticisms and suggestions which, I feel sure, have greatly improved its value. He supplied me with much of the factual material, and has allowed me to incorporate some ideas or statements drawn from his most extensive knowledge. Unfortunately, he will not allow me to make proper acknowledgment at the appropriate places.

Although I owe a very great deal to these books and discussions and criticisms, this book is ultimately based on more than seven years' experiences and encounters, on the love and friendships and quarrels and misunderstandings and delicate negotiations and casual incidents which made up my life in the United States. Some may think that a book such as this is poor thanks to a country and a people who have given me so much, but they will be those (few, I hope) who do not see the spirit in which this book has been written. Lest there be any misunderstanding, I will state categorically that I believe that the future peace and prosperity of the world depend on the mutual understanding and fruitful collaboration of the English and American peoples and governments, and that such understanding and collaboration are our only safeguard against the inconceivable horrors of another war, or the horrors, only slightly less grim, of totalitarian domination. But mutual understanding cannot endure if it is founded on delusions and falsifications; it must be based on the acceptance of our widely differing characters and ways of looking at and interpreting the world. This book is an attempt to contribute to such an understanding.

G. G.

---

[a] This ignorance about England has been remedied, at least in part. See my *Exploring English Character* (Criterion Books, New York, 1955).

I

EUROPE AND THE
REJECTED FATHER

THE AMPHIBIOUS assault on Sicily in July, 1943, marked the significant re-entry of the Western Allies into Europe. Still untried American armies took part in this campaign, and, just before the landing was made, the American general commanding one of these armies, the late General Patton, had an order circulated to his troops to raise their morale and impress on them the significance of the occasion. This order read in part:

> When we land, we will meet German and Italian soldiers whom it is our honor and privilege to attack and destroy.
> Many of you have in your veins German and Italian blood, but remember that these ancestors of yours so loved freedom that they gave up home and country to cross the ocean in search of liberty. The ancestors of the people we shall kill lacked the courage to make such a sacrifice and continued as slaves.

The public style of the late general was unusually flamboyant; but these three sentences have condensed epigrammatically a great number of psychologically significant truths about Americans.

". . . these ancestors of yours . . . gave up home and

country . . ." Whether the overriding motive which had driven those immigrants across the ocean was an ethical love of freedom, or a more material desire for greater opportunity, a better standard of living, or free land is unimportant in the present instance; what is significant is that most of the ancestors of most of the men under General Patton's command had come from Europe, had given up home and country, had rejected the values and traditions in which they had been reared, and had seen their children grow up to accept quite different values and traditions as their own, and to scorn and reject whatever European habits and ways of thinking the immigrant had unwillingly retained.

In 1860 the population of the United States, immigrant and native born, white and Negro, young and old, numbered a little over thirty million. In the seventy years that followed, just on thirty million European immigrants crossed the ocean and became Americans. What proportion of the hundred and eighteen million white Americans (the figure of the 1940 census) are descended from ancestors who had arrived before 1860, and what from ancestors who had arrived after, cannot be determined with any exactness; but it is worth recalling that whereas the resident population was composed of all ages, the immigrant population consisted predominantly of young people at the age of greatest fertility.[1]

". . . these ancestors of yours . . . gave up home and

---

[1] In 1940 about eleven and a half million white Americans were foreign born and twenty-three million were of foreign-born parents (Statistical Abstracts, 1945).

country . . ." With few exceptions the immigrants did not cross the ocean as colonists, to reproduce the civilizations of their homes on distant shores; with the geographical separation they were prepared to give up, as far as lay in their power, all their past: their language and the thoughts which only that language could express; the laws and allegiances which they had been brought up to observe; the values and assured way of life of their ancestors and their former compatriots; even to a large extent their customary ways of eating, of dressing, of living. Most of them escaped at the same time from discriminatory laws, rigidly hierarchical social structures, compulsory military service and authoritarian limitation of the opportunities open to the enterprising and of the goals to which they could aspire. But the rejection of home and country could not be piecemeal; the supports had to be abandoned with the restraints; individually the immigrants had to try to transform themselves into Americans.

Unless they had immigrated as children, or had quite exceptional psychological plasticity, this self-transformation was impossible in its entirety. Culture is strong and pervasive, and the national character which is the embodiment of a local culture is acquired above all in the earlier years of life; will power alone is not enough to modify those motives and ways of viewing the universe which spring from unrecognized and unconscious sources; the majority of mankind cannot remold themselves by taking thought. Consequently the greater number of immigrants, though they had rejected as much of Europe as they could, were still incomplete Americans; their own persons, their characters, their ways of thought, usually their accent, carried the stigmata of the Europe they had rejected. But though they could not transform themselves, their children would be transmuted; the public schools, in some cases aided by the neighbors, would turn their children into the hundred per cent Americans they could never hope to be themselves. And when this transmutation had taken place the parents themselves would be rejected as old-fashioned, ignorant, and in significant ways alien. The more successful the immigrant father was in turning his children into Americans, so that they had no other allegiances or values, the more his foreignness became a source of shame and opprobrium, the less important did he become as a model and guide and exemplar. Whatever her language and ways, the mother retained emotional importance as a source of love and food and succor; but to grow up to be like the father, to do no better than he had done, to be the same sort of person as he was, would be failure indeed and would be so regarded by the father as much as by the son.

It is this break of continuity between the immigrants of the first generation and their children of the second generation which is to my mind of major importance in the development of the modern American character, which gave rise to what might be called, by analogy with genetics, the American mutation.[2] It is true that in nearly

[2] There is some evidence for thinking that true genetic mutations also occur with some regularity. F. Boas' pioneer study *Changes in Bodily Form of Descendants of Immigrants* (Washington, D.C., 1912) maintained that there were statistically significant differences in such anthropometric characteristics as skull shape between people born in the United

all other parts of the world and in many periods individuals have changed their country of allegiance and have seen their children acquire characters and adopt values which were alien to them; but in these other cases the numbers of immigrants were insignificant in proportion to the populations of their host countries, whereas in many areas of the United States, particularly in the cities, they greatly outnumbered the older Americans; in the other cases the rejection of the father as a guide and model was a private solution to a personal problem; in the United States it was also an act which symbolized the acceptance of the dominant values of the society to which they had pledged allegiance. The individual rejection of the European father as a model and a moral authority, which every second-generation American had to perform, was given significance and emphasis by its similarity to the rejection of England by which America became an independent nation.

Modern history offers no easy parallel to the psychological and political conditions which accompanied the separation of the American colonies from England in the second half of the eighteenth century. Until a bare thirteen years before the Declaration of Independence and the outbreak of war the allegiance of the colonists to England seems to have been unquestioned. In local matters they were mostly self-governing, but they con-

States and their elder brothers and sisters born in Europe. The tendency was described as toward uniformity, long heads becoming rounder, and round heads longer. Later workers, however, it should be mentioned, have questioned the validity of Boas' statistics, and also his methods of sampling.

sidered themselves loyal subjects of the king of England, on a par with his subjects everywhere. Their outlook, their institutions, their philosophy and their religion all stemmed from England; the variations from the norm were no greater than those between one English region and another; the impact of novel foreign ideas (in particular French) was not greater in America than in London.

Between 1763 and 1776 this allegiance was destroyed for a significant number of the colonists by a series of arbitrary and high-handed acts on the part of George III and some of his ministers, which placed the colonists in an inferior position compared with the other subjects of the king, in that taxes were levied on them, troops quartered on them, and their commerce interfered with, without their consent. These departures from English practice were resisted in the name of English principles; when the recognized legal methods of obtaining redress were rendered fruitless by the blind obstinacy of the king and his ministers, the colonists, still acting on English precedent, took to arms to defend "the rights of Englishmen."

In the course of a protracted and often desperate war the allegiance to England was thrown off by the greater number of the colonists, including the most influential. This throwing off of the English allegiance was the rejection of the only embodied authority which was generally recognized; it was not, in those years, the replacement of one authority by another. The birth of the American republic was signalized by the rejection of authority as such: authority was coercive, arbitrary, despotic, morally wrong.

For eleven years the thirteen independent colonies pursued often mutually contradictory policies, linked only in a powerless voluntary confederation; but the almost complete bankruptcy to which this near anarchy brought the Confederation showed that it was impossible for them to survive without some sort of central authority; and in 1787 a Constitutional Convention was held to devise a federal government which would have the minimum of authority necessary for the independent survival of the United States. The remarkable document which was the outcome of these deliberations—the American Constitution—is especially noteworthy for the ingenuity with which authority is jealously circumscribed; the system of checks and balances and the principle of divided powers were intended to erect insuperable legal barriers to the excessive authority of one person or group.

In some significant ways the birth of the American republic can be compared with the mythological scene which Freud imagined for the origin of civilization and the institution of totemic observances. In Freud's "Just So" story the downtrodden sons combine together to kill the tyrannical father; then, overwhelmed by their crime, and fearful that one of their number will attempt to take the murdered father's place, they make a compact which establishes the legal equality of the brothers, based on the common renunciation of the father's authority and privileges.[3] England, the England of George III and Lord

[3] S. Freud, *Totem and Tabu*, 3rd edition, 1922.

North, takes the place of the despotic and tyrannical father, the American colonists that of the conspiring sons, and the Declaration of Independence and the American Constitution that of the compact by which all Americans are guaranteed freedom and equality on the basis of the common renunciation of all authority over people, which had been the father's most hated and most envied privilege.

This is of course only an analogy derived from a parable, but it does symbolize a number of major psychological truths. From the emergence of America as an independent nation two major themes appear as characteristic of Americans: the emotional egalitarianism which maintains that all (white American) men are equal to the extent that the subordination of one man to another is repugnant and legally forbidden, equal in opportunity and legal position; and the belief that authority over people is morally detestable and should be resisted, that the suspicion that others are seeking authority cannot be too vigilant, and that those who occupy the necessary positions of authority within the state should be considered as potential enemies and usurpers. The prized equality of Americans was and is dependent on the weakness of their government.[b]

As the immigrants' children learned to become one hundred per cent Americans in school, these lessons were impressed upon them continuously in their classrooms, in their lessons and textbooks in history and civics, in the sermons and celebrations which mark the patriotic cycle of holidays. For these children of Europeans the England of the textbooks became a monster of oppression and tyranny, and the throwing off of the English allegiance was stripped of nearly all the ambivalence which had accompanied the historical act; to reject authority became a praiseworthy and specifically American act, and the sanctions of society were added to the individual motives for rejecting the family authority personified in the father; and the father, with his European character and upbringing, was often excessive in his demands for obedience. But whether the individual father hindered or helped his children to become a different sort of person from what he was, was a question of minor importance; the making of an American demanded that the father should be rejected both as a model and as a source of authority. Father never knew best. And once the mutation was established, it was maintained; no matter how many generations separate an American from his immigrant ancestors, he rejects his father as authority and exemplar, and expects his sons to reject him.[4]

Psychoanalytic theory was developed in Europe; and, with the prevalent European social and family structure, it seemed reasonable to maintain that the positions of authority in the state—king, priest, policeman, officer, and so on—were symbolic extensions of the authority of the father. But this statement was based on the unjustified assumption that family forms and the role of the parents were identical everywhere, that all fathers everywhere were awe-inspiring figures of authority. A more valid generaliza-

[4] Margaret Mead has established that the modal American position today is third generation. See *And Keep Your Powder Dry*, Chapter III, "We Are All Third Generation."

tion would be that in any given society at a given time the patterns of authority in different situations tend to resemble one another, that in different contexts the emotional concomitants of superordination and subordination remain similar and interact on one another; the father models his behavior on that of the examples of authority in his society in much the same way that the child interprets social representatives of authority in the light of his attitude toward his father. When an American becomes a father he inevitably tends to maintain his role in a fashion congruent with the values of his society; his biological superiority to the newborn child is adapted to the patterns society gives for proper behavior in positions of superiority.

The typical American attitudes toward authority have remained substantially the same as those manifested by the framers of the American Constitution: authority is inherently bad and dangerous; the survival and growth of the state make it inevitable that some individuals must be endowed with authority; but this authority must be as circumscribed and limited as legal ingenuity can devise; and the holders of these positions should be under constant scrutiny, should be watched as potential enemies.

These attitudes toward the concept of authority over people and toward persons placed in positions of authority are basic to the understanding of American character and American behavior. They are far more than political; they are therefore quite different from the situations in, say, Ireland or Greece where to be "agin the government" is a recognized and respected political position, but where the authority of the church in the one case, and that of the family in the other, generally remains unquestioned. With the rarest exceptions, these attitudes do not involve the abstract idealism of the philosophical anarchism of Spain or nineteenth-century Russia; despite the political implications, they are above all moral: people, or institutions, who "push other people around" are bad, repugnant to decent feelings, thoroughly reprehensible. Authority over people is looked on as a sin, and those who seek authority as sinners.

The implications of these attitudes are manifold, and reach into nearly every sphere of American life. Thus the least respected and most suspect professions are those which, by their nature, involve the exercise of authority over other people—politics and, in peacetime, military service. People who enter these professions for any reason except to improve their social position or to make money are deeply suspect. There are a few families, predominantly from the South and Southwest, in which an officer's career is quasi-hereditary; but the main body of professional officers come from the graduates of West Point and Annapolis, and the appointment of candidates to these institutions is an act of political patronage performed by the congressmen and senators—who have the legal right to make such recommendations—for the poor but deserving sons of their supporters. A young man of ability who, without either such an appointment or any family tradition, announced in peacetime his intention to become an officer in the services would be very much looked at askance.[c]

Politicians are not suspect if it is believed that they have gone into politics for their own personal advantage, to make money or to improve their position. This is considered normal and understandable, a business on the edge of legality, similar to bookmaking or bootlegging in a dry state; it is not praiseworthy or particularly respectable; but provided the law is not too grossly flouted, there is considerable convenience in having available people who will "fix" one's traffic tickets, get jobs on the public payroll for one's more feckless relatives, see that contracts for public works go to the right firms. There is no general or widespread moral condemnation for the political "machines" which dominate most of the big cities of the United States, just as there was no widespread moral condemnation of bootleggers; many people would prefer to be without both, but the stability of society is not thought to be threatened by either. Since law, and the politicians who must administer it, represent a facet of authority, the general American attitude is riddled with ambivalence; it would be desirable if others were law-abiding, and if politicians were impervious to others' appeals; but one should not be inconvenienced oneself, nor submit tamely; and it is foolish to vote for a man who will never do one a reasonable favor. Walt Whitman's advice to the States, *Resist much, obey little,* is otiose in the case of most individuals. It follows that the exposure of the flagrant corruption of some senators in recent years was not greeted with surprised indignation; the general attitude seems to have been rather the resigned fulfillment of expectation; what else could one expect? And their corruption was at least a reassurance that they were in politics for what they could get out of it, and not for sinister reasons.

A person who goes in for a political career for reasons other than direct personal advantage is deeply suspect; he is perhaps secretly lusting after authority, and the greatest vigilance must be exercised to see that he does not gratify this sinful craving. It was, I feel sure, this moral attitude which lay behind the almost pathological hatred felt for the late President Roosevelt and his family by so many of the most respected and respectable Americans. A variety of rationalizations was given for this hatred, but even where they were not self-contradictory, they were most of them patently false; the hatred, however, was real and deep enough. By the less assimilated and less assured groups in the population he was loved like a father, and felt to be a protective, benevolent authority; [5] the remainder saw only the authority, and the fact that Roosevelt obviously did not dislike his position; and consequently, whatever he did or omitted to do, he was felt to be a menace.

This attitude toward the individual in supreme authority poses an inescapable dilemma which may help to account for the alternation of strong and weak presidents, noted by Harold Laski.[6] A strong president represents a moral threat; a weak one, even if he or his associates are not corrupt, brings the country dangerously near anarchy, for the careful provisions of the Constitution prevent any other group from exercising his necessary authority.

Government entirely by self-seekers, or by "businessmen" translating their search for profits into another

[5] In its intensity this dependency on the part of the socially insecure is a very recent development.

[6] H. Laski, *The American Presidency* (Harper, New York, 1940).

sphere, is not a practical proposition, however reassuring such a concept would be. The government itself must necessarily have some authority, and the people in the higher positions must therefore be tainted with this sin. This concept of moral contamination helps to account for the generally contemptuous attitude of Americans toward their government, whatever the group in office: the government is apart from them, is thought of as "they," practically never as "we." The government is apart from the people, its interests are different from the interests of the community; the main aim of the government is to increase its authority and the main duty of the public is to resist this. Some government is, admittedly, necessary; but the citizens should be vigilant to see that it is kept to a minimum. Government is a necessary evil; commonly, more emphasis is put on the evil than on the necessity. It is naturally not respected. In conversation and in writing the metaphor most commonly used to describe the proper role of government is that of the umpire in some sporting event such as boxing or baseball; the umpire is not to make the rules which have already been laid down (in the Constitution) nor to take part in the contest which is the real object of the exercise; the umpire's duty is merely to prevent one of the contestants from taking an unfair advantage of the other. In American sports, especially in baseball, the umpire is not respected; he is frequently challenged, and occasionally threatened by the players, and most freely insulted by the partisan spectators. Nevertheless, it is the "umpire" aspect of the American government which meets with the least suspicion and contempt; the Supreme

Court and its members are seldom suspected of improper attempts to increase its or their authority.

This is the only portion of the government which is not so suspected. Any attempt to increase government authority is met, at least in the initial stages, with the greatest moral indignation and resistance. This is particularly obvious in the case of proposed government planning. Preference for "private enterprise" represents no reasoned belief in the superiority of one method of production or distribution over another; it is not necessarily a screen behind which personal interests and hopes for profits are defended; it is a deeply sincere, quasi-religious moral attitude, as little susceptible to rational argument as the Hindus' aversion to killing cows. Since the resistance to government planning is fundamentally moral, each case has to be refought. The Tennessee Valley Authority is perhaps the most successful example of large-scale planning the world has yet seen: the desert has been made to blossom, great wealth has been added to the country, devastating floods have been controlled, whole populations are leading richer and healthier lives, and the enterprise is financially solvent; one would have thought the case for the unified control of rivers passing through several states completely proven. But the case for the proposed Missouri Valley Authority has to be fought all over again; no precedent can alter the fact that the extension of authority is inherently evil, and to be resisted.

It is this hatred of authority which makes America a nonmilitaristic ("peace-loving") nation. The connection between the readiness of individuals to fight and the readiness of societies to go to war has been assumed rather than proved; but to the extent that such considerations are relevant, American men do not show a marked distaste for fighting or violence. Margaret Mead [7] has outlined the rules which *should* regulate the occasions for fighting: the challenger should not strike the first blow, and the attacked should not be markedly smaller or weaker than the attacker. Boys in the country and in small towns who are validating their manhood sometimes walk around with a literal chip of wood balanced on their shoulder, the sign of a readiness to fight anyone who will take the initiative of knocking the chip off. And besides such ethical and friendly fighting, violence and the threat of violence do play a significant, often a major, role in American commercial, industrial, and political life. The violence of lawlessness has received excessive emphasis through the newspapers, the books, the films and the radio stories devoted to the gangsters and hold-up men; although such activities are less frequent than the publicity they receive would suggest, they nevertheless do occur. The rule of the political machines is often maintained by violence as much as by fraud; up till recently employers used the greatest physical violence to prevent the establishment or increase of trade unions; today many trade unions hold or increase their membership by the use or threat of physical violence; nonconforming business and professional men are frequently kept in line by the same threats. In their professional and political lives many American men have been forced into conformity by fear of physical violence. Al-

[7] *Op. cit.*, Chapter IX, "The Chip on the Shoulder."

though morally disapproved of, there is a general sneaking admiration for people who can "get away with" such methods; but greater and more public admiration goes to the victim of violence who "can take it," who withstands mistreatment with courage and equanimity; the practice of the Plains Indians, whose admiration was given to the man who would face death by torture with a song on his lips, has some echoes in the practices of the people who now inhabit their lands. An increasing number of public entertainments, especially radio shows, are built around the public humiliation of the amateur participants; and a regular feature of the American "tough guy" detective story is the physical sufferings of the hero.

No, Americans are not antimilitaristic because of a general withdrawal from fighting and violence; they are antimilitaristic because they detest authority; and military service today inevitably involves discipline, involves being pushed around and ordered about by officers. Conversations with returning veterans reveal almost invariably a far greater and deeper animus felt against their own officers than against the enemy, even the Japanese who during the war were regarded as inhuman. In the fantasies brought to light in psychiatric interviews pride of place went to those in which the officer was retaliated upon, humiliated, snubbed. Perhaps the commonest fantasy of all was that the soldier, again a civilian, was an employer and refused a job to the officer, also now a civilian, humble and suppliant.

This fantasy reveals in part the subtle distinction made between authority and power. Control over people—

authority—is always morally bad; control over things, or abstractions envisaged as things (natural resources, goods, services, money, chattels)—power—is morally neutral and even, within certain ill-defined limits, highly praiseworthy. This distinction is more an emotional than a strictly rational one; in the G. I. dream reported above, the life of the ex-officer was being effectively interfered with, but negatively, by exclusion, not positively, by compulsion. The great socioeconomic upheavals in American public life have occurred when it is suspected that legitimate power is being transformed into illegitimate authority: in the early years of this century in the attacks on the big capitalists, then personified by John D. Rockefeller and crystallized in the antitrust laws; currently in the attacks on the powerful trade-union leaders, personified by John L. Lewis and crystallized in a number of antilabor laws. The point where power becomes authority (or risks doing so) is apprehended rather than defined; it is a phenomenon of size.

Because of the possibility that power, especially great power, may be transformed into authority it is imperative for those in positions of great power to manifest in their persons the absence of authority, or the desire for authority. They must be conspicuously plain citizens, with the interests and mannerisms of their fellows; whatever their private temperament they must act as "one of the boys," glad-handed, extravert, mindful of first names, seeing their subordinates in their shirt sleeves and with their feet on the desk, democratically obscene in their language, with private interests, if any, simple and within the reach of all.

It can be argued that it was failure to achieve such a public personality that alienated John D. Rockefeller (until he acquired the skilled services of Ivy Lee) and still alienates John L. Lewis from the American public to a far greater degree than any of their peers in power.

If the powerful will not accept this unauthoritarian role, they may well have it thrust upon them. Few incidents are more revealing than the one in which J. Pierpont Morgan —powerful, austere, withdrawn—was photographed, after he had been testifying to a Senate committee, with a smuggled midget thrust upon his knee. From any rational point of view the incident was comparatively meaningless, the photograph merely incongruous; but that it had deep emotional significance is shown by the elation with which the photograph was hailed and the fact that it is still glee-fully remembered after the passage of very many years, and even after Mr. Morgan's death. What had the photograph effected? It had not reduced by one jot or tittle Mr. Morgan's financial power, which many people had con-sidered dangerous; but it had at least momentarily made Mr. Morgan look ridiculous; it had lessened his resem-blance to a figure of authority; a surprised-looking man with an elderly midget on his knee is no figure to inspire respect or awe.

Respect and awe are the usual emotional responses to personified authority, and are therefore among the most painful emotions that the Americans recognize, and are as carefully avoided by them as the feeling of shame-faced-ness is by the Japanese. In the face of people or situations which might evoke such feelings every effort is made by the use of levity, incongruousness, or elaboration to reduce them to a status where such feelings will no longer be appropriate.[d] Perhaps the most conspicuous and almost clinically perfect examples of such reactions in literature are Mark Twain's *A Connecticut Yankee at King Arthur's Court* and *Innocents Abroad*. The gossip column, the candid camera, the literary profile continue on the day-to-day level the more prolonged efforts made by debunking books; and a happy symbol of the attitude was the photograph, reproduced in nearly every American paper and every American newsreel, of the G. I. who, the day after the capture of Rome, climbed onto the balcony of the Palazzo Venezia and imitated Mussolini haranguing the crowd. The political implications were probably nil; here was a symbol of authority reduced to the level of every American mother's son.

Similar reasons, among others, lie behind the quite excessive interest that Americans pay, and have paid for so long, to the married life of the Duke of Windsor, and the amount of space that was given in the press to the marriage of Princess Elizabeth. This is not, as some naïve foreign observers assume, due to any devotion to the British Royal Family; it is rather the reducing of potentially awe-inspiring characters to the most human level.

Similar feelings are also a component in the virulent political anti-Catholicism of many Americans. In recent years this has only risen once to the surface—in 1928, when a Catholic was Democratic candidate for president—and it is usually for political and business reasons kept muted, the Catholics representing nearly a sixth of the total population, and probably the best organized group; but it is always present and capable of being tapped; it is not confined to pathological bigots dressed in night shirts. The Pope is the one person in the world on whose knee no midget can be popped, who cannot be involved in an amorous intrigue, whom one cannot slap on the back and call "Harry."

After the Pope, Stalin was probably the human being least susceptible to such humanizing treatment, the most difficult to represent as just like anybody else; but during the war, when good relations with Russia were desirable, American correspondents developed quite an elaborate family life for "Uncle Joe," including a rumored love affair, and—happiest touch of all—revealed that the tobacco he preferred in his inseparable pipe was a common commercial American brand, available to all at the corner drugstore.

In this connection it is worth recalling the intensity of the moral disapprobation that the Americans felt for the awe and respect which the Japanese manifested toward their emperor; this "emperor worship," as it was called, was felt to be the direct antithesis of democracy; and it was with an almost holy glee that newspaper reporters and public-relations officers set about reducing Hirohito to the status of an ordinary man in the eyes of the Japanese (or at least so it was hoped) as soon as it was politically safe to do so. The refusal of the American government to allow this to be done during the war was the cause of the most bitter acrimony and suspicion; and although the event fully justified such self-denial, some of the individuals believed to be primarily responsible for such a policy have had no further role in the American government.

The distinction between persons and things is also valid for the feeling of awe. Awe directed toward people is always painful and reprehensible; but awe directed toward things, or abstractions regarded as things, is tolerable and in some cases mandatory. The Flag, abstractions such as Freedom and Democracy, certain buildings and places connected with the earlier history of the United States— for example the Liberty Bell, the Lincoln Memorial, the Alamo—are all fit objects for awe and reverence. Awe is also a natural concomitant to notions of great size.

During all his formative years the young American has continually impressed upon him the proper attitude toward authority, and toward men who try to exercise it. Consequently, when he in his turn becomes a father, he finds his proper role toward his children defined and limited by the negative sanctions against the exercise of authority by one man over another. Even if his temperament made him tend toward dominating his children and exacting unquestioning obedience from them, he would get no support from his wife, his neighbors, or his community.[8] To a certain extent the pattern of authority in the state is reproduced in the family: it is as if the father represented the Executive, the mother the Legislative, and the neighbors, headed by the schoolteacher, the Judiciary authority. The child is in the position of the public, play-

[8] According to the New York Department of Welfare the most common reason given by unmarried mothers for their delinquency is their revolt against parental, and especially paternal, authority.

ing off one authority against another, invoking the system of checks and balances to maintain his independence. Although this is a somewhat far-fetched comparison, it more nearly represents the structure of the ordinary American family than does the patriarchal picture derived from Europe, or the mirror image of that picture, with the father's authority transferred wholesale and unaltered to the mother.

The picture of the actual structure of the American family is further confused by the English or European origin of many of the social forms, of much of the law, and some of the religion of the United States. With the exception of the very poorest Negroes, the form of the family is still patriarchal; children still take their father's surname, though the use of the mother's maiden name as a middle name is increasingly common; women have only recently gained full civil and legal equality, and most of the conspicuously honorific positions are still reserved for men. But although the forms are similar, the content is very different from the patriarchal societies of most of Europe and Asia.

The crucial experience of the second generation when the son was transformed into something the father could never be dominates the relations and expectations between all American fathers and their sons. Even if he is not an incomplete American, the father is almost by definition old-fashioned, unaware of the latest fads and fashions which occupy his children, ill at ease among the newly popularized gadgets with which they disport themselves. He is not, or at least not for long, a source of knowledge greater than his children can possess. Like the immigrant father, he does not expect his sons to be like him, to have the same sort of profession or stay in the same social class. His pride and justification depend on his sons' surpassing him and leaving him behind. Except for his fundamental maleness, the father is not a model on which the son is expected to mold himself.

The role of the father has been defined negatively. What is he positively? Above all, he is, or should be, the breadwinner of the family, exerting all his efforts to give his children a better education, a better "background," a better chance, than he had himself; to provide his children with the possibility of surpassing him is his great and principal function. He can and should give his children the occasion to improve their position vis-à-vis the neighbors' children, by giving them the possibility of boasting of his power: "My pop is bigger, stronger, richer, cleverer than yours." He should be a "buddy" to his sons and help train them in the specifically masculine techniques of fighting, sport, hunting, and the like. He should support and exemplify the moral precepts and rules inculcated by the mother and the schoolteacher.

As far as this final desideratum is concerned, there is a fairly consistent discrepancy between theory and practice. Once the sons have passed early childhood, there very often develops an open conspiracy between father and sons to thwart or sidestep the feminine rules of domestic and social behavior: "Don't let your mother catch you" is the code phrase by which such conspiracies can be recognized. The happiest relationships between American fathers and sons seem to be based on this shared masculine resistance to feminine demands and exigencies. In less happy families, this solidarity is broken by rivalry between father and son, tacitly in earlier years for the mother's regard and affection; more openly at adolescence and after for the use of the family car, the choice of T V program, the use to be made of other conveniences or gadgets which father and son must share. In such contests the father is generally the loser. The commonest way of referring to one's father is "my old man." America belongs to the young.

With the notable exception of the New York *Times* almost every American newspaper carries comic strips, usually at least a page of them. They are one of the few important bonds (the films being another and the presidential elections a third) uniting nearly all Americans in a common experience. As one moves away from the big cities and the Atlantic seaboard, the space devoted in the newspapers to international, and even national, news becomes less and less, and that given to local happenings increasingly greater. But practically no newspaper is so provincial that it does not carry the nationally syndicated comic strips. As one travels about the country one may be unable to learn what is happening in Congress or at the United Nations meetings; but there is no excuse for ignorance of the latest adventures of Superman, Li'l Abner, Joe Palooka, Skeezix Wallet, and the numerous other protagonists of these synthetic fantasies.

One of the earliest and most popular of these strips, and one which is still continuing today, is entitled *Bringing up*

Father. In its ideas and execution this strip seems today old-fashioned and overfantasticated, though Jiggs and Maggie still have their devoted followers. A more revealing commentary on current attitudes to the American family is *Blondie. Blondie* is one of the few strips—*Gasoline Alley* is the only other one that I know of—in which time is allowed to play a role, in which the characters grow up and grow older, marry and have children. Because of the admission of time, these strips have a realism absent from the other timeless fantasies and reflect, though naturally with considerable distortion, many of the shared patterns of American life. *Blondie* consists of a series of disjointed and comic episodes in the domestic life of a self-possessed, good-looking, neatly dressed middle-class woman. She is married to Dagwood, an untidy office worker who has to run every morning to catch the bus from his suburb; he is generally incompetent, inefficient, greedy (he is always sneaking into the kitchen to make the most incongruous sandwiches), sensuously lazy (outside the office and the kitchen he spends much of his time trying to take a nap on the sofa or laze in a hot bath), generally good-tempered and easygoing but given to sudden and completely ineffective rages. In the earlier years, the comedy chiefly derived from the skill with which Blondie saved them both from the results of Dagwood's blunders. After a few years of marriage, their union was blessed with issue; first a son, Alexander, the image of his father, and more recently a daughter, Cookie, favoring her mother. When I was separated from the Dagwood family, Alexander was a schoolboy, and many comic situations arose from his increasingly successful rivalry with Dagwood.

Although naturally exaggerated, Dagwood does represent a very widely spread attitude toward the American man as husband and father. Dagwood is kind, dutiful, diligent, well-meaning within his limits; but he has so completely given up any claim to authority that the family would constantly risk disintegration and disaster, if it were not for Blondie.

[b] The constantly repeated phrase "creeping socialism" is the current term to designate the feared strengthening of government power. See Postscript p. 255.

[c] This paragraph about the esteem of military and naval officers in peacetime is no longer valid.

[d] An almost clinically perfect example of this attitude was the fantastic popular success of the gramophone record "The First Family" in the last months of 1962 and the first of 1963. The section in which President and Mrs. Kennedy were depicted as being alone on a Saturday night, peeved at not being invited to a desirable party, was particularly indicative.

II

MOTHER-LAND

AMERICA is commonly represented by two images, two icons. One is an extremely thin, tall old man, his gray beard trimmed to an old-fashioned goatee, his clothes of a by-gone era embellished with the stars and stripes of the national flag, the other a portly maternal female dressed in flowing robes of classical style (which still do not differ too greatly from the ceremonial costumes worn by matrons at such functions as weddings), crowned with a diadem, and holding a torch in one hand. These two images are used alternatively in poster, cartoon, or medal to represent the United States; as far as I know there is no accepted rule as to which icon should be used in which circumstances; and consequently the choice, as it is commonly practiced, is the more revealing.

Uncle Sam represents above all the government of America, chiefly in its demanding aspects, occasionally ne-gotiating, rarely giving. Uncle Sam is to the fore when sac-rifices or deprivations are called for: Uncle Sam wants you, or your boy, in the army; Uncle Sam wants your savings for war loans; Uncle Sam wants your money for taxes; Uncle Sam wants you to use the telephone, or transport, or electricity less, for the sake of the war effort. This is his most constant role, the embodiment of a despised government in its most unpleasant and interfering aspects. More rarely he is shown in cartoons as negotiating with other government figures and, shrewd old yankee horse-trader as he is pictured, almost inevitably being cheated, robbed, or swindled by his companions. Occasionally Uncle Sam gives handouts of "the people's money," either to undeserving foreign nations or to special groups of Americans, sometimes deserving, such as veterans when they receive a bonus, more often parasitic, such as artists and dancers and the lazy supported by W. P. A. Incidentally, I remember few caricatures of Uncle Sam as benefactor to the deserving; it occurs more commonly as a figure of speech in the talk of the recipients, who may feel some uneasiness about their right to this unearned increment.

This summary (and certainly partial) description of the functions of Uncle Sam will account for the very negative attitudes most Americans have toward this figure. It has amused me to ask a great number of Americans the symbolic relationship of Uncle Sam to themselves. None have admitted that Uncle Sam represents some feature of themselves, and the greater number deny any kinship with him, despite the use of the term "Uncle." His clothes date him, and the contemporary ancestors of most Americans were not Yankees. He is unrelated, neither loved nor respected, but at best grudgingly obeyed. Government must needs come, but woe to him through whom government cometh.

In far different case is the Goddess of Liberty. She is America the bountiful, pouring out endless treasures from her cornucopia. She is America the Land of the Free, holding high her torch to illuminate the path to democracy for the benighted. She is America the Land of Opportunity, yielding her favors to those who are industrious, energetic, and ingenious enough to deserve them.

The history of the Goddess of Liberty—Liberty Enlightening the World—as an idol is not without interest. She arrived fairly late in America, in 1876, to mark the centenary of the United States as an independent nation. She was a gift from the people of France (who, incidentally, are the only major nation who habitually represent themselves with a feminine icon, Marianne) and was designed by a passionate admirer of America, the Frenchman Auguste Bartholdi; as a model for the Goddess he used his mother, Charlotte Beyser Bartholdi. She was set up on Bedloe Island outside the port of New York with her back to the land, facing the ocean, the first significant sight to greet the arriving immigrant or returning traveler. Inside her pedestal was inscribed a most beautiful and resounding promise of maternal solicitude and welcome, a promise which has been unfulfilled during the last twenty-odd years.[1] She has become an object of sight-seeing for pro-

[1] This promise is in the form of a rather informal sonnet, entitled "The New Colossus." The most famous lines are the last five, which read:

> Give me your tired, your poor,
> Your huddled masses yearning to be free,
> The wretched refuse of your teeming shore,
> Send these the homeless, tempest-tossed, to me.
> I hold the lamp before the golden door.

The authoress, Emma Lazarus, was always interested in Promised Lands, but apparently changed her mind about which land was promised. Some twenty years after writing this sonnet she became one of the leading Zionists.

vincials visiting New York; she is hollow inside and tourists may scramble up her and peer at New York and its harbor through the slits in her diadem. She is not one of the objects or places which demand awe and reverence; rather is she treated with familiarity and love. New Yorkers never visit her, except under protest, accompanying a "country cousin."

I have not dwelt on the implications of these two figures out of pure love of iconography. They represent, in the shorthand of symbolism, a most important psychological truth. America in its benevolent, rich, idealistic aspects is envisaged (by Americans) as feminine; it is masculine only in its grasping and demanding aspects. The American land itself—Columbia in an older iconography —is feminine; its possession has been on occasion wooing, on occasion seduction, and on occasion rape.

This female aspect of the United States did not immediately spring up fully developed, like Pallas Athene from the head of Zeus; it is a process which has grown over time, and the end of which is not yet in sight.

The previous chapter outlined the moral rejection of authority in general, and that of paternal authority in particular. Consistently with this view the child should grow up without any authority at all (and attempts have been made to achieve this goal in some of the more fanatical progressive schools) but in practice this has proved impossible. Completely undisciplined, untrained children are too much danger to themselves, and too much nuisance to the parents. The ideal of a childhood completely free from overt authority is perhaps attained more nearly in the

United States than in any other Occidental nation; but some authority there must be, some agent who will reward good conduct and punish bad; and, almost by default, the role of the father having been so diminished, these functions have been, in largest part, taken over by the mother.

The patriarchal role of the father toward his small children has always been a social artifact, for the infant is biologically dependent on the mother and she is sufficient to caring for it. But human beings do not lead purely biological lives, and in most societies the father plays an important role in training the children, particularly the sons, in rewarding approved and in punishing disapproved behavior. In few societies is the role of the father more vestigial than in the United States.

The contrast between the social role of the father and the biological role of the mother in all societies probably helps to account for the relatively dominant position of the mother in the American family. In the crucial second generation, when the social role of the father was so greatly diminished both by his deficiencies as an American and by the prevailing attitude toward authority, the biological importance of the mother was to a great extent maintained. She might be as old-fashioned and tainted with European ideas as the father; but these drawbacks could not interfere with her provision of care and succor and food and love. The mother could not be rejected as the father had been, nor did public attitudes demand that she should be; and so the mother became the dominant parent in the American family, almost, as it were, by default, rather than by any demands on her part for excessive privilege or influence.

Various other historical explanations—such as conditions on the expanding frontier and the absolute scarcity of women during significant portions of American history —have been given for the unquestioned high position and far-reaching influence of women in contemporary American society. These may have been contributory causes, but they are certainly not sufficient. After all, these conditions are not unique. To go no further afield, the conditions were very similar in nineteenth-century Australia and New Zealand but the results are not the same.

The fact that the American mother has arrogated to herself, or has had thrust upon her, the dominant role in the rearing of her children—a role which is held by the father, or shared by both parents, in most other societies—has far-reaching results on the character of the children; and, since this situation is not a novel one, on the character of the adults also.

The means by which a moral character, influenced by ethical considerations, is formed is now fairly well understood. In those societies which develop a moral character, parents (or parent substitutes) train children to an ethical viewpoint by giving love and rewards when the children conform to arbitrary moral standards, and withdrawing love and inflicting punishment when the children fail to conform.[2] By the process of anticipation the children learn

[2] This method of training children is not universal, nor even very general. In many societies parents maintain an even attitude toward their children, using the neighbors or the wrath of imagined or impersonated supernaturals as instruments of discipline.

to act toward those moral standards as if the parents were present, giving or witholding love, rewarding or punishing, when they are absent; the children act as if they had taken into themselves the approving and disapproving aspects of their parents. This internalized control becomes part of the total personality; it is called by the psychoanalysts the superego, in common speech the conscience.

The idiosyncratic feature of the American conscience is that it is predominantly feminine. Owing to the major role played by the mother in disciplining the child, in rewarding and punishing it, many more aspects of the mother than of the father become incorporated. Duty and Right Conduct become feminine figures.

This makes the role of the daughter, herself to become a mother, particularly easy and straightforward, and helps account for the perpetuation of the situation and the notable ease and assurance of the American woman. But for the son, the American male, the situation is far more complicated and confusing. He carries around, as it were encapsulated inside him, an ethical, admonitory, censorious mother. In all the spheres where moral considerations are meant to operate—and in America this means above all in relations between people—men act as though they were being guided by (or rebelling against) rules and prohibitions enunciated by a moral mother. For the mother—actual or internalized—not only gives her sons rules for proper behavior in the spheres in which she and her kind play a role; she also sets rules for behavior in spheres to which she and her sex have no entry. Margaret Mead [3] has

[3] *Op. cit.*, Chapter IX.

detailed the way in which the American boy is taught *when* to fight (but obviously not *how* to fight) by his mother, and how he has to try to reconcile her injunctions to be peaceable and to stand up for himself. Similarly she demands that her son should be a success, but is incapable of saying how he should achieve this. Her rules and categorical prohibitions are extended to such spheres as male sexuality and drinking.

The fact that the rules for moral conduct are felt to emanate from a feminine source is a source of considerable confusion to American men. They tend to resent such interference with their own behavior, and yet are unable to ignore it, since the insistent maternal conscience is a part of their personality. This frequently leads them into seemingly contradictory behavior, and is a major source of the bewilderment which most non-Americans feel when confronted with American men.

A second result of this state of affairs is that all the niceties of masculine behavior—modesty, politeness, neatness, cleanliness—come to be regarded as concessions to feminine demands, and not good in themselves as part of the behavior of a proper man. As such they become irksome and are sloughed off—with relief but not without guilt—whenever a suitable occasion presents itself. In peacetime such suitable occasions are stylized: the stag poker game, the fishing trip, the convention, the class reunion; during the war the armed services not only permitted but demanded the abandonment of most such domestic taboos; and the conflict between the demands of male society and the insistence of the encapsulated mother's voice was most often the greatest cause for conflict, not seldom ending in psychoneurosis, in the newly enlisted youth.

Although insistent and peremptory, the authority of the maternal conscience is neither absolute nor terrifying in the majority of cases; it is felt to be tempered by love and understanding, and susceptible to wheedling and deceit to a greater degree than is customary with a paternal conscience.

The original impetus to the adoption of a feminine conscience and a feminine standard of values is given by the mother; from the age of six onward it is given further reinforcement by the fact that in the United States schoolteachers in the primary and secondary schools are overwhelmingly women. The role of the schoolteacher is far more important in the United States than in any European country; besides imparting knowledge, she is the arbiter of disputes and the guide and emblem of proper American conduct. During the period of the great immigrations it was above all the schools which turned the children of foreigners into little Americans; the judgment of the schoolteacher was accepted by the child, and usually by its parents, as the true guide to proper American conduct; the schoolteacher was the fountainhead of Americanism. Even though the proportion of second-generation Americans is now much lower (except in a few urban areas) the position of the schoolteacher as the guide to proper conduct still remains very high; [e] she is more up-to-date and "scientific" than the parents. In the nineteenth century, when the country was constantly expanding, a very large and significant proportion of the teachers were young women from New England; and it is through their influence that the puritan ethic (never part of the religious belief of more than a small proportion of the population) received such widespread public endorsement.

In the case of second-generation Americans, whose family still reflected some modification of the European pattern, the teacher was psychologically particularly important, for it was only by following carefully her precepts that one could become a proper American and shed the stigmata of foreignness that made one's parents a source of shame. When this was the only voice incorporated it was harsher and shriller than that of the mother, for it was not felt to be tempered by love.

Except in deviant families and among the snobbish rich (who send their sons to boarding schools, fondly thought to be constructed after English models) most boys reach and pass adolescence under almost undiluted female authority; their conduct has been regulated by female norms; praise and blame, their ratings in the competitive world of childhood have almost all been given by women; it is small wonder that their conscience should become predominantly feminine.

The manifestations of the female conscience in public life give rise to the peculiar behavior which Americans call "idealism"; this is the proclaiming of moral rules of conduct which other people should follow. "Idealism" is not, at least in the first place, a standard which guides one's own conduct; still less is it the setting of an example for others to copy; it is the laying down of rules for the conduct of others which need not apply to oneself. It derives directly from the situation where mother and teacher lay down instructions and prohibitions for the boys they are rearing, without either group feeling that these rules apply to the person who enunciates them.

The one major domain where the voices of the mother or the teacher—actual or internalized—are seldom, if ever, heard is in business and in activities which are thought to be part of business, such as a great deal of politics; this is because business is conceived as dealing primarily with things, and only incidentally with persons. The world of things is thought of as a peculiarly masculine domain, outside the realm of feminine morality; and a great deal of the animus felt and expressed by businessmen and their spokesmen against the New Deal was due to the fact that its social legislation was felt to be introducing into the domain of masculine privilege the meddling female morality.

The fact that there are spheres in American life to which moral rules do not apply is disconcerting to the more consistent moralists, to the extent that they let themselves be aware of this. But the more general reaction is simply to deny the existence of such spheres. There is a general and concerted tendency to ignore those aspects of the universe which clash too strongly with the general ethical picture. This system of achieving morality by treating as nonexistent facts which cannot be reconciled with an ethical picture reached its most consistent development in Christian Science, as originated by Mary Baker Eddy. The system of Christian Science is particularly congruent with feminine American morality. This basic attitude has had fairly wide diffusion over many spheres of American life, particularly perhaps in the treatment of death. The elaborate art of the morticians, the cosy beauty of the funeral parlors, and the landscaping of the gardens of rest have attempted to remove from death most of its poignancy, and most of its meaning; for death is too absolute a challenge to hedonism to be accepted and integrated. An increasing number of films and magazine stories have as their plot the replacement of a lost dead one by another just as good. Another aspect of the same attitude appears in the great number of euphemisms employed in polite conversation and writing. What morality cannot control it tends to ignore.

Besides their role in the formation of the American conscience, American women play a most important part in the American social and economic scene. "Never underrate the power of a woman" is the slogan of a prolonged advertising campaign of *The Ladies' Home Journal*, illustrated by cartoons which show in ever varying settings how the woman's choice prevails over that of the man with her (presumably her husband). The advice is valid.

Market researchers, whose business demands that they be accurate in such matters, reckon that women make more than three quarters of the retail purchases in the United States. This means that there is practically no sphere of design, from men's neckties to automobiles, which does not cater in the first instance to women's taste. And even where women are not in fact the more important consumers they are often treated as if they were. Thus independent research has shown that in America men go to the movies in just about the same proportion as women; but Hollywood's important film producers still mainly act on the belief that they have to please a predominantly feminine audience.

It has also been stated, though I do not know how the figures were arrived at nor how accurate they are, that women control over three quarters of the investment capital in the United States. One explanation may possibly be the greater natural longevity of women, coupled with the often early death of overdriven tycoons; another may be the discrimination in favor of women shown by many laws regarding property; in some states, notably California, the partiality is certainly excessive.

American women reach their greatest social influence from the time they near the menopause. As mothers and housewives, almost always without servants, the first twenty years of their married life (after, perhaps, a short period in the "younger married set") are perforce, in the vast majority of cases, overwhelmingly domestic; but when their youngest child has safely passed adolescence they can devote themselves to wider duties and pleasures. Americans typically marry early and have their small families [f] (outside the farms) soon after marriage; and consequently a woman will have completed her expected role as a mother while she is still in vigorous early middle age.

The expected role of a mother is finished when she has brought her children, as healthy and as high principled as possible, to the end of their formal education. After their final graduation (in most cases some time between sixteen and twenty-one, though there are occasional extensions in both directions) the children should have achieved complete independence, ideally leaving the maternal home, and usually the town in which they were reared, and setting up on their own. The mother is not expected to play any part in her daughter's marriage, beyond possibly being an honored guest (even though she be technically the hostess) at the wedding reception; she does not entertain for her adult daughter, though she should have provided entertainment for the friends of her adolescent children while they were at school.[4] As a grandmother she can feel vicarious pride in her grandchildren and give them presents; but she cannot help her daughter in their upbringing, for pediatrics—this is the impressive term given to the rules for rearing children—will have completely changed since she herself was a mother.

Her role in the life of her graduated son should be, if possible, even more negative. The son should pass her, leave her, revere her, and forget her. As Margaret Mead has acutely pointed out, Mother's Day (a day in late spring, determined and announced by the President, and most assiduously promoted by the retail merchants who advertise even the most incongruous gifts as suitable "For Mother") is a Day of Atonement in which formal restitution is made for the previous year's neglect.

This complete withdrawal is the ideal; but for a significant portion of the women the future outlook is too

---

[4] Conspicuous entertainments for adolescent daughters are given by rich and socially ambitious parents who provide them with a public "debut."

bleak, without love beyond the long accustomed love of the husband, no longer rated as sexually desirable by anybody, too self-respecting and afraid of the neighbors to employ a gigolo, even if they live in an area where such are obtainable; and these cling to their children, particularly their sons, longer than society considers fitting.

The clinging mother is the great emotional menace in American psychological life, the counterpart to the heavy domineering father in England and on the Continent. Many books and plays have been written in which she is the villain (the late Sidney Howard's *The Silver Cord* is a particularly telling example), she has been made the object of shrill diatribes, such as Philip Wylie's *Generation of Vipers*, and psychiatrists have written books to prove that she is the main, and sufficient, cause for nervous breakdowns or psychoneurosis among recruits to the American army.[5] This picture of the clinging mother, and the fear of such vampirelike possession—the hidden fear that one may oneself have been so possessed—is one of the components in the very strong ambivalence American men feel toward women.

However, most American mothers do not cling exces-

[5] *Their Mothers' Sons* by Edward A. Strecker, M.D. (New York, Lippincott, 1946). The above was written on the basis of reviews, but I have since read this fantastic book. According to it, Mom, the clinging, possessive mother, not only causes psychoneurosis, she is the main cause of every unpleasant social phenomenon, from schizophrenia, through lynching, to National-Socialism and Japanese Emperor worship! Written by an American and for Americans, this book gives considerable implicit confirmation to my main arguments. Reading it, one would almost think that Americans were produced by parthenogenesis, so vestigial is the role given to the father in the family or in forming his children's characters.

sively, just as most European fathers are not excessively
domineering; instead they turn their energies to social and
cultural ends. This is a very unusual social phenomenon.
In nearly all societies, primitive and complex, European
and Asiatic, nonprofessional married women in their fifties
and sixties are of little importance in the social scene, influential at most in their domestic spheres and through the
pressure they can bring to bear on their male relatives; in
America this group is one of the most active and influential body of citizens, as well as one of the most conspicuous.

It is easy enough to laugh at these middle-aged women,
with their eager seeking after knowledge and wisdom,
their dogged clinging to stylishness and a falsely youthful
appearance, their naïve approach to the arts and to gra-
cious living (a key phrase), their façade of almost excessive
self-assurance so often a protective front to the deepest uncertainty and humility, the high seriousness with which
they view themselves as paladins of Civic Virtue and ar-
biters of the world's destiny. They were held up to ridicule
week after week in Helen Hokinson's drawings in the *New
Yorker* and in the works of her numerous imitators in that
and other journals and papers. American films, advertisements, radio, popular books and magazines barely admit
the existence of women between the ages of twenty-five
and seventy ("Mother" in the Mother's Day advertisements is usually either so youthful that she must have
been married at twelve to have children of gift-giving age
or so old, wrinkled, and decrepit that Whistler's Mother
seems like her younger sister), but when the middle-aged

clubwoman does appear she is nearly always a figure of fun, in the films amusingly caricatured by Billie Burke, Mary Boland, or Marguerite Dumont. It is these women who make up the usually despised audience (and pay the extremely generous fees) for European and American lecturers, eagerly and seriously drinking in the words and noting the personality of celebrity and notoriety, scientist and quack, priest and swami, poet and prophet, explorer and desk-strategist, best-selling novelist and worst-selling painter; earnestly, though perhaps with inadequate discrimination, they turn out week after week, month after month, occasionally dragging their protesting husbands with them, hungering and thirsting after wisdom and taste. It is these women who filled (and will fill again) the ocean liners, the big hotels, the conducted tours, scouring the rest of the world for the art, the tradition, the romance they felt that they lacked at home, buying artistic souvenirs at outrageous prices and outraged at the way they have been cheated (an occasional supposed bargain is sufficient recompense), loudly complaining when, as inevitably happens, they fail to find the sanitary, gastronomic, and other conveniences which even a small American town would provide, benevolently ready at the drop of a hat to correct and reform their backward hosts, paying generously and ungrudgingly, and getting little value for their money.

Yes, it is easy enough to laugh at these women, for there is some deep incongruity between their matronly appearance (emphasized by their overyouthful clothes and make-up) and their undergraduate (almost schoolgirl) eagerness and seriousness; but they cannot be dismissed with laughter. They are, many of them, civically conscious and conscientious; they are imbued with genuine, if often provincial and impractical, idealism, untainted with the amorality of the male world of business; if they are convinced of the rightness of their cause they will give their time, money, and energy unstintingly; and if business considerations do not appear to be involved, they will be able to enroll their husbands. When, in recent years, corrupt local political machines have been put out of office, when bad local conditions have been improved, the impetus in many cases has come from the relevant women's clubs. Women's clubs are now listening, as never before, to self-styled experts—often the most lamentable charlatans and vicious propagandists—on world affairs, the United Nations, and the atomic bomb; and it is in the women's clubs that the future policy of America, and so in many ways the future of the world, is to a great extent being decided.

Outside the United States this assertion will seem a paradox, for, as I said earlier, no other society gives an important public role to the mothers of grown sons. In the United States, perhaps because of the failure of Prohibition (the most conspicuous effort of the women's clubs so far), they are seldom taken as seriously as they merit. Other groups are more vociferously and publicly, in the short run more effectively, interested in politics—the Political Action Committee of the Congress of Industrial Organizations, the shrill "liberals" of *P. M.*, the *New Republic*, the *Nation* (more influential than their minute circulations would suggest), "veterans" organized as pressure groups, the old-established political parties; these groups, and others like them, have a direct impact on the day-to-day development of politics. But in all these groups the voice of America's feminine conscience is confused (one might say contaminated) by masculine calculations of profit and loss, by the search for individual or sectional advantage, so that America seems to speak with two voices, the one proclaiming high ideals, the other negating them with the most unenlightened self-interest. But from many of the women's clubs the voice of America's conscience rings out clear and serene, as it were double-distilled; for it is the mothers themselves speaking, and at the same time the encapsulated mothers who are the conscience of all Americans.

It hurts our dignity to think that our future is being determined by Helen Hokinson's grotesques, by the women with the monotonous, insistent voices who are dissatisfied with their bathrooms or prosaically enthusiastic about a piece of real old-world architecture, by Madam Chairman; but one might easily be in worse hands. They are ignorant and know it, and spend much time and money to lessen their ignorance; they are ludicrous and sometimes secretly suspect it; they are usually unlovable and unloved, and this they find hard to admit; they are profoundly provincial, and of this they are profoundly ignorant. But many of them have high principles; and if these principles are sometimes confused and impractical, making too little allowance for human weakness and material difficulties, they are seldom mean or self-seeking;

and these principles are not easily deflected by propaganda, however cunningly devised, though they may be confused by specious special pleading. These principles may not foreshadow a world of freedom and ease and adventure, for the voice of the schoolmarm is too insistent. But they are our chief bulwark against chaos. Without them we might well be left with a subcontinent of cynicism and hedonism—a civilization where "anything goes," where everybody gets his, where business and politics, law and order all become unscrupulous rackets; where the only purpose in life is to get enough money, by whatever means, in order to pursue happiness, but only capture pleasure; where sobriety is too painful and meaningless to be endured and alcohol [g] shows the way to a joyless good time. In most of the big cities in the United States this picture is dangerously near realization; it could capture the country; its nihilistic progress is held back by the tightly corseted figure of Madam Chairman, by the pinched and overeager schoolmarm. They are the present embodiments of the Goddess of Liberty.

[e] For current fears about schoolteachers, see Postscript, p. 257.

[f] The typical size of American families has increased in the last fifteen years.

[g] Narcotics should now be included. See Postscript, p. 249.

III

THE ALL-AMERICAN CHILD

EVEN before Hitler annexed Austria and drove Freud and his followers into exile, the theory and practice of psychoanalysis were more widely spread and widely accepted in the United States than in any other country. In the last ten years its diffusion, both directly and in various dilutions, has been very great. Americans have employed the insights derived from psychoanalysis in a number of novel situations, but there have been no major consistent theoretical innovations. However, in the process of becoming a naturalized American, as it were, one important aspect of Freud's original theory has been sloughed off, treated as almost nonexistent; all postulates about the inborn wickedness of the child—its aggressive and sadistic "instincts"—have been abandoned, sometimes by rationalization, sometimes merely by default. In American psychoanalytical thinking, the child is born faultless, a *tabula rasa*, and any defects which subsequently develop are the fault of uncontrollable circumstances, or of the ignorance or malice of its parents who mar what should otherwise be a perfect, or at least perfectly adjusted, human being.

This is an interesting example of the way in which even the most intractable material will be modified until it is congruent with the major psychological emphases of a society; no theory could gain widespread acceptance in America which did not concede that the child was the hope for the future, and that he could, given the proper start in life, go further and fare better than his parents. This belief is basic in America; it probably gained its original impetus in the crucial second generation, when the child was to become the complete American the parents could never be; and it has been maintained by the best-beloved American myths and exemplars—from log cabin to White House, from newsboy to millionaire, from the ghetto to the Supreme Court, from slave to institute head. It only needs the proper upbringing to develop these potentialities in every newborn child.

But what is the proper upbringing? Ah, there's the rub. In all societies except the United States, and, to a lesser degree, the countries facing her across the Atlantic, at all periods except during the last hundred years, the answer could be given without hesitation: the proper way to bring up children is the way we were brought up. Whether the child was weaned at three months or three years, whether it was tightly swaddled or allowed complete freedom, whether it should be trained to cleanliness at the earliest possible moment or left until it could walk and talk, whether it should be allowed to crawl or be prevented from crawling, whether it should be sung to and cuddled or kept firmly apart from any contact with other people and refused all show of affection—these alternatives were simply not envisaged. There was the correct way of rearing children, and that was the end of it. When a woman bore her first child, she had the accumulated wisdom of her whole society to help her; the grandmothers, the midwives, the neighbors all spoke with one voice; every baby she had seen since she could first notice anything was being brought up in the same way; her path was clear. Of course there were individual variations, mothers who spoiled their children more, or were more severe to them, than was called for; but they were relatively narrow variations from a common pattern; and the pattern itself was unquestioned.

In America the situation is very different. Here again the second generation was crucial; the girl's mother's advice was suspect, for was it not tainted with the backwardness and superstition and unsanitariness of the old world? And even if she were inclined to follow it, there would probably be endless clashes with her husband and his mother who may have followed quite a different set of rules from quite a different country in Europe. And so they sought the American way to turn the whimpering bundle of beet-red flesh into the future president of the United States, the future dean of a women's college; they consulted the expert.

In the best mercantile tradition the demand created the supply, and experts on child rearing appeared in enormous numbers and of every degree of qualification. There were the dieticians, who gave advice as to how to make the baby as big (husky) and healthy as possible, there were the psychologists who gave advice as to how to make the baby as happy as possible, there were the disciplinarians who gave advice as to how to train the baby as early as possible, there were the romantics who gave advice as to how to keep the baby as uninhibited as possible, there were the medical men and the medicine men, the good plain quacks and the good plain crooks. The government itself was not indifferent to the demand and, through the Children's Bureau of the Department of Labor, put out pamphlets distributed by the million to tell young mothers how to bring up their offspring. These pamphlets are completely revised every few years; a comparison of the different editions gives an interesting synopsis of the vagaries of the most accepted theories of child rearing.

How any given child was or is reared depends on a concatenation of quite fortuitous circumstances—what doctor the mother consulted during her pregnancy, what was the success of a given method on the child next door, what she had been taught in school or college, the impact left by advertisements of "scientific" baby food, the books or pamphlets she had recently read. A mother need not bring up all her children in the same way; a change of doctor or of locality, a novel lecture or a new magazine article, dissatisfaction with the first born, may all decide her to try something different, more modern, more scientific, with the next baby.

In societies where the raising of children is patterned and consistent, detailed scientific investigation has always shown a clear and significant correspondence between the vicissitudes undergone by the young child and the most striking shared aspects of the adult character and the form and emphasis of the main institutions. What becomes of this theory if it is only by chance that two Americans have been brought up in the same way?

Despite the very great difference in practice—the extent of the difference can hardly be exaggerated—there are important regularities in the upbringing of American children which are as determining in the formation of adult character as the patterned practices are in other societies.

One of the most important of these regularities is the attitude of the mother toward the upbringing of her baby. Whatever system she may be following, she can never have the easy, almost unconscious, self-assurance of the mother of more patterned societies, who is following ways she knows unquestioningly to be right. The American mother is always more or less anxious, anxious lest she make mistakes or forget part of the prescribed routine, anxious lest the baby should not respond properly, often anxious lest she should after all have chosen the wrong method. Usually this anxiety does not show on the surface, but is transformed into a set of psychological symptoms which are technically known as compulsive. The rules which have been accepted for the upbringing of the particular child tend to acquire an almost magical force, so that a lapse or alteration becomes a sin, and not merely a mistake.

Whatever the system by which infants are cared for, the most important and insistent aspect of this care during the first few months of their life must be their feeding. Whether the baby be breast or bottle fed, whether it be given orange juice, cod-liver oil, spinach water, mashed vegetables, or distilled water, it must be fed at least several times a day. Feeding is anyhow the most intense pleasure, as far as we know, that a baby can experience; for the American baby the importance of feeding is enhanced by the compulsive anxiety with which its mother regards its "schedule" and its "formula," the distress which is manifested if by any chance the infant does not absorb the proper amount of nourishment which the system has allocated to its age and size. For all human beings the mouth with its functions is the most important organ of the body in the first months of life; but with maturation, as other portions of the body come under control, it loses its paramount position as an organ of pleasure and power for most people in most societies. For most Americans, however, its importance as an organ of pleasure and power remains very great, in extreme cases arrogating functions more suitable to other organs; and this importance is in great part determined by the very great importance which the mother's compulsive anxiety gives to her infant's oral activities.

Besides the pleasure of satisfaction from feeding, there is also the pain from hunger when food is denied; and this experience can also, and perhaps even more effectively than satiation, give exaggerated importance to the mouth's functions. Most American babies experience acute hunger. Some of the earlier "scientific" methods of child feeding actually induced malnutrition, with a heavy incidence of such diseases as rickets; but such gross miscalculations are mostly of the past. However, all but an eccentric minority of child-rearing systems have as a most important component a feeding schedule; they lay down rigidly at what times the baby shall be given what foods; the baby's hunger is to be regulated by the clock.[1]

This is perhaps inevitable in an urban society almost completely without maids or nurses; unless the child were trained to a fixed routine it would be too difficult for the mother to get through the rest of her duties. But this is a novel and unnatural arrangement, for clocks are a fairly recent invention diffused over only a small part of the globe; during the greater part of history, and for the greater part of humanity today, the baby's feeding has been regulated by the autonomous rhythms of the baby's hunger, whether the child be fed at the first symptoms of hunger or only after it has made the whole neighborhood ring with its cries. But a feeding schedule pays only the grossest and most statistical attention to the baby's autonomous rhythms; there is no little clock inside the baby which determines that the baby shall get hungry when, and only when, the schedule says it shall be fed.

Most babies accommodate themselves fairly quickly to whatever schedule is imposed upon them, but there is usually a period before this is successfully accomplished during which the baby screams with unassuaged hunger and rage, and is not fed. Because of the compulsive attitude adopted toward the training system of which the schedule is such an important part, most mothers feel it would be *wicked* to advance the bottle half an hour or give a supererogatory spoonful of sieved carrots. However nerve-racking or heart-piercing the baby's screams may be,

[1] In progressive circles this pattern has recently started to change and such babies are now fed on "self-demand."

it is far better for the baby to let him wait till the right time; it would be mere self-indulgence to quiet his screams. And so most American babies learn to experience hunger, and the fear of hunger. When they grow up this fear remains with them, though disguised and taking irrational forms (as do all infantile fears which survive in adults); symptoms of it can be seen in the frequently expressed fears that America will be reduced to want, perhaps to actual starvation, if it lets its food or resources or money outside the country,[2] by the quite excessive anxiety induced by an unbalanced national budget, by the fear of depletion in any of its possible aspects.

Relevant to this point also is the very great erotic fetishist value given to women's breasts in contemporary America; they have almost overtaken the earlier value given to legs. As a stimulating sight, well-separated and well-developed breasts under a tight-fitting overgarment are thought to surpass almost any amount of nudity. Film stars have made their reputation through tight sweaters; one film, *The Outlaw*, made a national reputation and had a running battle with the various censorship bodies because of the emphasis given to the heroine's bosom; and in many war factories women workers were forbidden to wear sweaters because of the resulting distraction and inefficiency. The cleft which separates the breasts is almost the

---

[2] An outstanding example of this attitude can be found in an article published during the war in the *Reader's Digest* by the popular novelist Louis Bromfield; writing in August, 1943, he used all his skill and sincerity to convince the literate population of the United States that they would be actually starving by the coming February if the government did not change its policy!

greatest object of erotic curiosity; and a number of English films in which actresses wore Restoration costumes have been considered too indecent to be shown to the American public without fichus. The great addiction of most American men to milk as a drink has also probably symbolic significance.

Besides the wickedness of interfering with the baby's schedule, there are other acts connected with the baby's mouth which the mother, at least until recently, would be wicked to permit. It is wicked to let a baby suck its thumb, and even more wicked to give it an artificial comforter (pacifier). One "advanced" mother of my acquaintance who saw no harm in so indulging her baby had to give up taking it into the streets, she was approached so often by well-meaning strangers who wished to save her from the error of her ways, and the baby from the disastrous, if unclearly conceived, results. In the eyes of these well-intentioned women, my friend was not making a mistake in the way she was treating her child; by allowing it to suck too much, she was committing a sin, and willfully impairing its future health and happiness.

As the child grows up, the importance of food is, if anything, enhanced. Physical punishment for small children is generally disapproved of by white Americans; so good conduct in the children is rewarded by giving greater quantities of food which American children are expected to prefer, bad conduct by withholding it, or giving less. Fortunately for today's American children American science has stated that some of the foods which are regarded as rewards are good for children, so that American parents can indulge their children in candy and ice cream without any of the qualms which their own parents felt. Twenty years ago food that was good to eat was not good for you (and conversely) and if you overindulged your child you were undermining his morals as well as ruining his health. Today, in this respect, you can have your cake and eat it, and the implications are far reaching; the guilt which older generations of Americans manifest in the face of pleasure is almost completely absent among the young.

Some foods, then, become a sign of love and approval and, as such, take on an added symbolic importance. An illuminating sidelight on the importance sweet foods acquire can be found in the love names given by a parent to the child, and also by a lover to the beloved: honey, sugar, cookie, and so on. There are also a number of fixed phrases which are used in similar circumstances: "You are so sweet I could eat you right up." [3] There is, of course, another aspect to this equating of the loved person with loved food; to swallow means to incorporate, to take into oneself, but also to destroy; the mouth with its teeth is an instrument of power, as well as of pleasure.

Although sweet foods acquire perhaps the greatest importance, this does not mean that the rest of eating becomes unimportant when the child can take a mixed diet. The mother's compulsive anxiety is turned to making sure that her child has a properly balanced diet, according to whatever dietary fad or theory she believes in; and it be-

[3] *Time*, Atlantic Overseas edition, February 3, 1947, reports: "In Uniontown, Pa., a Paradise Restaurant customer looked Waitress Kathrine Gayd up and down, exclaimed, 'Gee, you're pretty—good enough to eat,' grabbed her hand, bit it."

comes of great emotional importance that the child shall take in sufficient quantities of the right foods. Certain foods are treated as if they had magical virtue, as if by swallowing them the child would automatically become big and strong and powerful: milk in the first instance, spinach (especially in the last generation: witness *Popeye, the Sailor*), orange juice, certain cereals, meat, lettuce, carrots; if mother's boy will eat the proper quantities of them he will grow up to be the strongest man in the world. As a consequence these foods, too, become of great emotional importance; the child can show its love for its mother by swallowing the recommended foods obediently; it can show its rejection of her, or manifest its independence, by refusing, or trying to refuse, the foods she so anxiously presses on it. "Feeding difficulties" is one of the chief causes for consulting child psychologists: to refuse food is to refuse mother's love, to refuse to grow up; it is, indeed, usually a sign of profound inner conflict.

A neurotic development of the mother's fear that her children will not eat enough of the magical health-giving foods can be found in the obese children who are relatively common in the United States and practically unknown elsewhere. Typical enough to be included in nearly every composite picture of American schoolchildren is the excessively fat boy (it is most frequently a boy), round like a butter tub, with the fat in creases all over his body. So exaggerated is the obesity that it was thought for a long time that the children suffered from some sort of glandular imbalance; but careful investigation of the homes from which these fat boys came showed that the explanation was simpler: they were merely being continually stuffed with quite excessive quantities of nourishing food. The anxiety of their mothers had lost touch with reality; to prove that they loved their children, and their children loved them, they plied them with food until they swelled up like balloons. As an added illustration of their loss of touch with reality, most of the mothers of these overfed children claimed in the first interview that their children ate practically nothing.[4]

The belief in the magical health-giving virtues of certain foods is avidly exploited by the manufacturers of breakfast cereals and other commercial foods; they spend lavish sums in advertisement campaigns, especially over television, directed at the children (not, be it noted, at the parents) to persuade them that they, too, will have superhuman strength, power, and resourcefulness if they persuade their parents to buy the advertised commodity. The superhuman All-American Boy is the protagonist and trademark of one such breakfast food.

This belief in the magical virtues of specific foods is carried almost unquestioned into adult life. Steak is not only typically a man's favorite dish; it contains, by the most obvious rules of sympathetic magic, virtues such as no other food can give: it provides red blood. To be deprived of steaks, as many Americans were during the war and in the autumn of 1946, during the butcher's strike against the government, is not merely to go without enjoy-

[4] See "Obesity in Childhood. The Family Frame of Obese Children," by Hilda Bruch and Grace Touraine, *Psychosomatic Medicine*, Vol. II, 1940, New York.

able meals; it is sapping the constitution and lowering the vitality of red-blooded men. Various other foods have specific qualities based on similar simple principles: thus oysters are aphrodisiac, lettuce leaves, or very thin slices of toast or biscuit, slimming, and so on. And although Americans enjoy the richest and most varied diet of any people on earth, possibly excessive for sedentary workers, millions supplement it by taking in addition vitamin pills in considerable quantities. The discovery of the vitamin seemed to give scientific validation to the belief in the magical quality of certain foods. Their diffusion has worked wonders in poverty-stricken districts in the South, where such deficiency diseases as pellagra were endemic. Outside these areas the diet was usually more than adequate, but the manufacture of vitamin pills quickly became a major industry, selling hundreds of millions of dollars' worth yearly.[5] Nearly every corner drugstore in every town has a counter devoted to these magic tablets. Advertising campaigns promise pep, energy, sexual prowess, business efficiency, and almost the gifts of Superman if you will only spend a few cents a day on their special proprietary brand.

There is less apparent uniformity in the other aspects of infant care and training than there is in their feeding, though the mother's attitude remains constant. In recent

---

[5] *Fortune* (May, 1945) calculated that in 1944 the retail sales of vitamin preparations amounted to $200,000,000—a third of all retail drug sales in the United States. Besides these retail sales of chemicals, about a quarter of this sum was spent by wholesalers who added vitamins to their products ("vitaminized" bread, milk, etc.) and nearly as large a sum again on cod-liver and halibut oils and similar natural substances, chiefly valuable for their vitamin content.

years most of the experts have tended to pay less attention than their predecessors to the early training in cleanliness; but the adult emphasis on sanitation and plumbing is so great that even if the mother conscientiously refrains from punishing her dirty child she will find it almost impossible to disguise completely her tenseness and disgust, and this communicates to the child almost as effectively as punishment. Infantile genitality, formerly treated with complete and horrified prohibition, is now viewed with indulgence in some, and constantly growing circles; but here again the mother's own deeper feelings may contradict her conscientious actions. The amount a baby is kissed and cuddled varies enormously, but it is usually less rather than more. There are some indulgences which are given to babies in other lands which are very seldom given to American babies; American babies are hardly ever swung or placed in a rocking cradle; they are carried very little; they are seldom given aids to teething.

Because of the great hopes placed on the baby, and because of the necessarily experimental manner in which it is being raised, the mother is anxious, from the very first, to find out if her baby is developing as it should. She has only one guide: comparison with the neighbors' children of similar age and social position, being raised on the same, or parallel, principles. The "science" of pediatrics is changing so rapidly that older children are no guide; they were raised under the disadvantage of old-fashioned, unscientific methods, and what may have been a good enough performance ten years ago may be quite inadequate now. And so from birth (the "correct" weight for a newborn child changes constantly, but there always is a "correct" weight) the child is placed in a competitive position vis-à-vis its age mates. The mother's pride in her child and her self-esteem as a mother depend on her baby's not falling below the average for its group. Its weight, its growth, its acquisition of bodily skills, its time of teething, its time of talking, are all points on the scale by which the baby's success is weighed. As Margaret Mead [6] has pointed out in detail, the mother's love is conditional on the child's success in this competition with its peers; only if it is successful can the mother give it her unconditional love, for it proves she has been a success in her role as mother, that she has done her duty by the hope of the future and can look the world in the face without shame. This does not, of course, mean that the failures in this primal competition are unloved or neglected; on the contrary, even more anxious attention may be paid to their getting the proper diet, to helping them to catch up; but the love for the failures is mixed with a sense of guilt; such children are a constant reproach to the inadequacy of the mother.

As soon as a child has acquired sufficient physical independence to be let out of doors alone—certainly by the age of three, and often earlier—it will leave its family and spend most of its time with its competitors and rivals in the immediate neighborhood. It will have known and played with these children (provided the parents have stayed in the same neighborhood all the time) from the time that it could be safely taken out of the baby carriage; but this earlier sociability has taken place under the

[6] *Op. cit.*, Chapter VI.

watchful and anxious eyes of the mothers. By the time the child is three the mother is likely to be occupied with a younger brother or sister; and even if she were not, even if she had complete leisure, she should be ashamed of keeping a constant eye on the child, keeping it permanently tied to her apron strings. By so doing, she would risk committing the greatest crime that an American parent can commit: she would risk turning her child into a sissy.

This concept of being a sissy is a key concept for the understanding of American character; it has no exact parallel in any other society. It has nowadays become a term of opprobrium which can be applied to anyone, regardless of age or sex; although it is analogous to some English terms of opprobrium (e. g. milksop, cry-baby, nancy, mother's darling) it is more than any of them. Schematically, it means showing more dependence or fear or lack of initiative or passivity than is suitable for the occasion. It can be applied to a gambler hesitant about risking his money, to a mother overanxious about the pain her child may suffer at the hands of a surgeon, to a boy shy about asking a popular girl for a "date," to stage fright, to overt apprehension about a visit to the dentist, to a little girl crying because her doll is broken, just as well as to occasions which directly elicit courage or initiative or independence and which may be responded to more or less adequately. It is the overriding fear of all American parents that their child will turn into a sissy; it is the overriding fear of all Americans from the moment that they can understand language that they may be taken for a sissy; and a very great deal of American speech and activity, so often mis-interpreted by non-Americans, is designed solely to avert this damning judgment. Particularly self-confident Americans may say "I guess I'm just a sissy . . ." when they feel quite sure that they are not. When applied to adult males (but only in that case) the term also implies sexual passivity.

To prevent this dread development, the American child is constantly urged toward independence and activity and initiative, greatly praised for every real or reported manifestation of these qualities, reproved or punished for failure. And its independent activity in the neighborhood playground is a first and most important testing ground.

This early introduction into social life away from constant parental supervision (the younger groups will normally be watched by one or two of the mothers) has a number of important consequences. First of all it presents the child with another source of authority, which it can oppose to and play against the parents. Few parents can stand against the plea of "Gee, I don't see why I shouldn't; all the other kids are allowed to," or even "John's [Mary's] mother lets him [her] do it and he's three months younger than I am." If one protects one's child more than the neighbors do, if one demands greater compliance, if one is more fussy, more anxious, does not one risk turning one's child into a sissy, or, at the very least, risk that it may be so regarded, and so taunted, by these neighbors' children, its playmates? Consequently the pace is constantly set for greater freedom, greater permissiveness, greater independence for the children. There is no absolute standard; what children of a given age are allowed or encouraged to do depends on the period, the region, the locality, the social standing and income of the parents; but what is consistent is the tendency toward greater permissiveness, greater freedom; the fiats and prohibitions of the greater number of American parents are constantly being overruled by an appeal to the authority and example of the neighbors. In this way each generation of Americans acquires in early childhood attitudes which will subsequently reinforce the belief in divided authority, the system of checks and balances, and the supreme importance of the neighbors as guides and exemplars.

With rare exceptions (as when an older brother or sister brings its junior along) the children of a play group are very much of an age, with a span of at most eighteen months to two years between the oldest and the youngest. This group of near equals is in many ways the primary group for Americans all their lives; it is against these that they must measure and prove themselves.

Although the parents no longer participate directly in much of the child's social life, the child quickly finds out that they have the keenest interest and anxiety as to how it is acquitting itself. The same competition is now going on, the same proving whether the parents have produced and reared a child up to, above, or below the average; but instead of the tests being scales or charts it is now the account that the child gives of its activities abroad when it returns home. So, from a very early age, the child finds itself a speaker before an attentive and appreciative audience of adults,[7] and discovers that what it tells produces praise or blame, love or the withdrawal of love. Again, a function of the mouth—speech—becomes of the greatest psychological importance. When the child starts to tell of its exploits and triumphs it is very small and weak, and its parents are, by comparison, very big and strong. To hold their interest, to extort their admiration and approval, the child inevitably starts to speak overemphatically, to exaggerate, to boast. The parents are so used to this (they did it themselves) that they allow it to go unchecked, mentally making the calculations which will separate the kernel of true achievement from the husk of infantile self-glorification and self-dramatization. Although as they grow up the disparity between the size and power of the speaker and the audience disappears, Americans tend to continue to talk about themselves and their accomplishments in the same manner as they did as little children; American audiences interpret this with ease; but non-Americans generally fail to, and consider it as excessive boasting and self-glorification—which it would be if they, with their quite different upbringing, spoke about themselves in the same terms and tone of voice.

In the crucial second generation there was the further complication that, in the majority of cases, parents and children had only a very limited vocabulary in common. The child's vocabulary was naturally limited by its years,

[7] See Gregory Bateson "Morale and National Character" in *Civilian Morale*, edited by Goodwin Watson (Boston, Houghton Mifflin Co., 1942).

that of the parents by the usual inadequacy with which un-trained adults use a foreign language they have acquired only in maturity. As a consequence, most of the subtleties of English syntax and vocabulary were lost; the most extreme and violent words and phrases were used to cover all gradations of meaning.

This heightened, over-dramatized, over-emphatic method of speaking is contagious; the child only half believes its own boasts and stories, and consequently only half believes what its parents say. To make the proper effect on their child, American parents must exaggerate in their turn, double the force and content of their threats and promises; a child only expects a portion of the promises (and practically none of the threats) to be carried out; but it is deeply mortified and disappointed if such promises are not made; it would suspect that it is not loved, not worthy.

This situation continues in some form all the time that the child lives in the parental home, and helps to account for the extraordinary importance given to *words* in American public and political life. Modern America is perhaps more than any other country actually built on words, on the words of the Constitution and the Declaration of Independence, and, behind them the Word of God. Because of the quasi-sacred character of the Constitution its words have had to be adapted to situations never envisaged by its drafters; the development of America, and consequently the history of the world, was profoundly modified by the judicial interpretations given to the words "due process" and "person" in the fifth amendment. The members of the Supreme Court should logically be lawyers; but a great many of the other major positions in the American government have gone to lawyers. And lawyers are after all people whose special skill lies in the cunning interpretation and manipulation of words. Lawyers, more than any other profession, have given America its presidents, headed by Thomas Jefferson, Abraham Lincoln, and Franklin Delano Roosevelt; of the thirty-two men who have been President of the United States, twenty had practiced as lawyers, two as judges, and two more had studied law but had not practiced. During recent years more than half of the members of both houses of Congress and of both parties have been lawyers; in some Congresses the proportion has risen to two thirds.[g] Despite the development of other means of communication, the estimation given to oratory (either as public speaking or lecturing) remains extremely high; many observers believe that the popularity of the late President Roosevelt was created and maintained above all by his skillful technique of radio oratory.[h]

Lawyers are not the only skilled manipulators of words who are honored and influential in American public life. The public-relations expert is a more recent, and therefore less honorific, profession than the lawyer's, but his impact on American life is great and growing. All that the public hears about the larger corporations, a very great deal it

[g] Dr. John Brown Mason (*Rocky Mountain Law Review*, Dec., 1937) worked out the percentage of lawyers in Congress between 1928 and 1936, the 71st to the 75th Congresses. In the Senate the percentage varied between 61 and 76 per cent, in the House of Representatives between 56 and 65 per cent.

hears about its government, almost everything it hears about its public figures—politicians, millionaires, film actors, and the like—come through public-relations experts (if they serve individuals they are often called press agents) who select and transform the available facts into the words most likely to please or titillate their public.

Advertisers are another very highly paid group of word manipulators, whose influence is enormous, though their prestige is not particularly high; and journalists yet another, whose prestige is extremely high, though their influence as a group is probably less than that of the advertisers. Journalists arrogate to themselves, and are accorded, a position of importance hardly paralleled in any other country; and the denial of the right to be able to say, or write, what one likes is probably seen as the greatest single menace of dictatorship. To a great extent foreign countries are rated by the facilities they give to American journalists; and journalists are generally considered more trustworthy witnesses than State Department officials.

But although words are so important, they are never taken quite at their face value; the child never fully believes its own stories, nor its parents' threats and promises. All statements are regarded with some skepticism; there is always some exaggeration, some hokum; spoken or written words are never thought to be the whole truth.

This skepticism is profound and all-pervasive; and it is most efficiently exploited. A special branch of journalism and broadcasting has sprung up which purports to give "the truth behind the news." Its two most notorious practitioners, Walter Winchell and Drew Pearson, have the biggest reading public and listening audiences of any regular writers or speakers in the United States, considerably greater than those of any writer or commentator who uses the public sources of news. Their technique is to write as though they were hidden under the desk, or the bed, while important decisions, political or marital, were being made, and then revealing to their audiences what the principals refused to divulge. "Reveal" is the key word with which they introduce their rumors, guesses, and facts. As gossips they help to reduce to the most human status figures who might otherwise evoke feelings of awe and respect; as political commentators they pose as champions of the public against the anonymous, authoritarian "they" in the government, daringly acquiring and republishing secret papers, thwarting the sinister plots which governments inevitably indulge in. They do get some information not available to the ordinary run of journalists; besides their regular informants, disgruntled officials and civil servants pass to them damaging information about their rivals, or details of political activities of which they disapprove; but even so their batting average is not high.[9] Both these journalists are liberal, well-meaning men, according to their lights; the harm they are doing to Americans would appear to be considerable, less on account of the rumors they float, for these are mostly quickly forgotten, than in the encouragement and enhancement of skepticism.

As well as the boasts, there are the promises. These, too,

[9] See the series of articles on Walter Winchell by St. Clair McKelway in the *New Yorker* of 1940. These articles were subsequently expanded into a book entitled *Gossip: The Life and Times of Walter Winchell* (Viking, New York, 1940).

find their parallel in American adult and political life in the very great emotional importance given to public statements of high intentions and high ideals. The Fourteen Points, the Kellogg declaration "outlawing war as an instrument of policy," the Atlantic Charter, are well-known international examples. Domestic ones are more frequent: the Fourth of July orations, the charters of various clubs and fraternal orders, the "platforms" on which, every four years, the major political parties seek the presidency. Any resemblance between the platforms, so eagerly and hotly debated, and the legislation introduced by the successful party is, in the words of the disclaimer which precedes American films and novels, purely coincidental; [10] but this does not mean that the platforms and other noble documents and promises are therefore unimportant. They signify a willingness to support such noble ends, and are therefore comforting, just as the parental promises, though not literally fulfilled, were a comforting sign of parental love and intention to reward. Americans feel cheated and disillusioned if such statements of high intentions are not made, just as the child felt its parents did not love it if they failed to make the expected promises.[11]

[10] The promises about the legal improvement of the Negroes' status, which have been planks in the platforms of both parties for a number of elections, are far from having been fulfilled by subsequent legislation.

[11] Relevant to this discussion is the American attitude toward the political independence of dependent peoples. On general principles, peoples should be independent as soon as possible, just as children should be independent as soon as possible. But beyond this general principle, the declaration of a subject people's independence is by itself of the utmost importance. By the treaty which was imposed on it, the Philippine Republic is as dependent on the United States economically, and has as little

So far, in discussing the upbringing of the American child, I have avoided sex pronouns and, somewhat awkwardly, used the word "it"; unfortunately English lacks a single word for he-or-she, and it would have been necessary to use the phrase all the time, for the treatment given small boys and girls differs only slightly in degree, not at all in kind. There is, however, an important difference in effect. As was pointed out in the previous chapter, all Americans acquire a predominantly feminine conscience; and this faces the little boy with a dilemma which his sister does not experience. Because of the encapsulated mother, the little boy has doubts about his masculinity, whereas the little girl is reaffirmed in her femininity. To prove to himself, and to the world, that he is a real "he-man" (the reduplication in the term is in itself suggestive) the little boy has to be more strident, shout and boast more, call more attention to himself than his sister need. American children of both sexes are brought up very similarly, by and large face the same dilemmas, and acquire the same type of character; but all the overcompensations for insecurity —and a great deal is demanded of American children, up to the limit of their powers—are far more developed in the boy.

The ideal American family consists of two children, an elder daughter and a younger son, generically known as "Sis" and "Buddy" (or "Junior"). This does not mean that this size of family, or order of birth, is statistically

freedom of action, militarily, as many of the colonies of other empires. But it has been declared independent; it is nominally free; and that, in the vast majority of American eyes, is infinitely more important than the actual facts of its subservience.

more common in the United States than in other countries
of similar urbanization; but this is the typical composition
when the average American family is pictured in illustration or advertisement, and very often in popular fiction
and films. In narratives a third child, a still younger
brother, is often introduced for dramatic effect.

In all societies everywhere the birth of a younger baby
involves the older child in considerable psychological tur-
moil, if for no other reason, because the new arrival inevitably displaces the older child from the center of family
love and attention. Different societies interpret this situation in different ways. Margaret Mead [12] has suggested
that the typical American reaction of the child to the newborn baby is one of resentment, because the new arrival
is permitted all the babyish ways which the older child
has had to abandon in its forced progress—up to the limit
of its strength—toward independence and adulthood.
From this initial situation she derives "the bitterness toward all those who 'have it soft', 'get by', 'get away with
murder', a bitterness combined with envy."

With the exception of a single combination, the relationship between brothers and sisters is without deep intensity. They have no special obligations toward one another (except to "agree," not to squabble too much); outside the rural South, the brother is not expected to defend
his sister's honor, nor is he responsible for her fortune, her
marriage, or her children. In the vast majority of cases
brothers and sisters scatter as soon as they leave home;
typically they follow different pursuits, live in different

[12] *Op. cit.*, Chapter VII.

localities, and, if they go to a university, go to different ones.

The one important exception occurs when two children of the same sex, particularly two boys, are born within a short interval of each other—at the most, two years. In this case the elder brother is likely to introduce the younger brother into his play group, and later his gang; and this has some regular and typical results. The younger brother is a member of a group in the majority older than he is, and with standards of daring and accomplishment beyond the level of his years. Fired by the standard he is set, the younger brother (the "kid brother") becomes extravagantly rash in his words and actions, confident that he will be saved from the dangerous results of his behavior by his older brother's protection, by his superior strength and wisdom. This situation is common enough to have several analogues in adult life. The most striking is to be seen in Congress, where the House of Representatives often acts most irresponsibly, in the confidence that its elder brother, the Senate, will save it from the worst aspects of its folly.

As the child grows in independence and skill, its father becomes somewhat more important, particularly as an authority which can be opposed to that of the mother. Most mothers conscientiously try to build for their husbands the position of authority in the family, and tell their children to ask his permission; but they often override his decisions, on the ground that he is too severe or too lenient, that he doesn't make allowance for children or that he is spoiling them. Most American parents dislike accepting the onus of restricting their children's pleasure and amusement; and there is a very general tendency for the parent first approached to put the burden of decision on the other. Most children learn this early, and become adept at playing one parent against the other. In those households where the father controls the children's pocket money, a refused application from the father will often be made good by the mother from her domestic budget. In many families it seems as though the parents were in covert competition for their children's love.

In the September adjoining its sixth birthday every American child will go to its neighborhood school, with the insignificant exception of the very rich. This may well be in a different town or district from that in which it was born, for conscientious American parents will often, within the limits of possibility open to them, move their home to that neighborhood whose school offers the best opportunities to their offspring. Schools are rarely judged by scholastic standards or opportunities, for, within a given region, the variation is slight. They are judged by their size, by the splendor and modernity of their buildings, by the number and condition of the accessory structures—workshops, indoor gymnasiums, and the like—and often by the absence of Negro children, or too many children of the alien and foreign born. The town in which an American spends the greater part of his schooldays is known as his "home town."

At school the competition for success, by which the child can earn its parents' love and approval and rate itself in the world, is again partly formalized. In American schoolrooms scholastic performance is classified on a five-point scale, usually from A to E, though marks are sometimes used, and these grades are inscribed on the report cards which the child must take home monthly. Since C is the average for the child's peers, parents can see immediately how their child rates in his year's crop of young Americans, whether he is a credit to them and himself, and therefore worthy of unqualified love, or whether they have failed in their most important function.

School athletics are less important for the rating of young children, and, in a way, never very important for the vast majority of American children. All American boys are expected to enjoy unformalized sports, typified by the baseball game on the empty lot; but to "go out for" a school sport means to accept a quasi-professional status, to acknowledge athletic abilities above the average. Athletes as a class are admired, envied, and privileged; they represent their school against its neighbors and rivals; and all boys, at any rate, are meant to follow the fortune of their teams with the greatest enthusiasm and emotional involvement. Among the athletes themselves the competition for success, symbolized by the Letter, is extremely keen. But it is a matter of individual choice whether the boy will himself enter in this competition; extra praise and regard are given to those who successfully do so; but blame is not given to those who do not.

In the event of an inadequately equipped athlete engaging in a competition beyond his powers, the attitude of the noncompetitors and of those he competes with are strongly contrasting. The people who are not involved in the competition are likely to identify with this valiant "underdog," to admire and praise his courage, and get great vicarious satisfaction from any success against the mighty that he may achieve. In contrast, the competitors have little respect for a person "going out of his class" and are justified in using all their strength and skill to eliminate him.

As was stated earlier, the children find in the school-teacher an authority who can nearly always be successfully opposed to the parents. The parents keep this acknowledged rival and superior under the closest scrutiny, demanding in her private life standards of conduct and moral rectitude far higher than those they apply to themselves or their neighbors. This supervision is formalized in the parent-teacher associations (P. T. A.) in which the most civic-minded parents meet with the teachers at regular intervals to discuss the school and their children. Though often in fact aided by grants from the federal or state treasury, the school is regarded as created and paid for by the initiative and taxes of the local inhabitants; it is their creation, and it is their duty to see that it compares favorably with its rivals. The American public school is justifiably one of the chief sources of American civic pride.

The American school is, in the first instance, a social device, and an extremely successful one, for stamping the American character on children, whatever their background and origins may be; it is only secondarily an institution for implanting and transmitting knowledge. Scholastic achievement is one of the few spheres where American children are not pushed to the limit of their strength;

compared with any country of Western Europe, the standard required at any given age is low. Most Americans attend school for more years than most Western Europeans, however. Classwork has a few distinctive features: training is given in public speaking by the use of recitations (spoken themes) as well as by essays; civics is an important subject, often made vivid by visits to neighboring factories, constructions, police courts, and the like; biology and science are taught early; study of the dead languages, if taught at all, normally only starts at high school (from the age of fourteen); European history is practically not taught at all; visual aids and recordings are frequently employed as adjuncts to teaching; vocational training starts early (again from high school) and is given in a great number of subjects, with very complete technical equipment in the bigger urban schools. Apart from this direct vocational training, American public-school education is less directed toward equipping the children for adult life (except for the development of Americanism) than toward making their childhood enjoyable and significant; under the influence of John Dewey, most American teachers believe that "children are people"; and much class time is given over to communal tasks and discussions with little direct relevance to later life.

The constant pushing toward independence, toward adulthood, is continued. Except for a few children of the protected rich, American boys are urged to earn, or at least supplement, their pocket money (spending money) by working after school hours. There are a number of jobs which are generally regarded as the special domain of schoolboys (except in a few states which have stringent child-labor laws): newspaper delivery in the first instance, often the delivery of groceries, the soliciting of subscriptions for, and the delivery of, magazines, mowing lawns in summer and clearing snow away from paths in winter, caddying at golf clubs, and so on. From high school onward these may be supplemented by other jobs: serving behind the ice-cream counter at a drugstore, tending furnaces, washing cars, and the like. Far from being stigmatized, these early gainful activities are universally approved; they are signs, not of parental poverty or stinginess, but of the individual's independence and self-reliance. Girls do not normally start earning as early as boys; but from high school onward they have varied opportunities for employment; of these the most general in recent years is "sitting," looking after babies or young children while the parents are out; by this means the girls simultaneously earn money (the job is well paid), demonstrate their independence, and get quiet and time for their homework.

When school starts, the mixed neighborhood play group typically gives way to gangs entirely or predominantly of one sex; and these gangs continue up to, and in some cases through, adolescence. The gangs may engage in almost any kind of activity compatible with the strength and interests of its members; but nearly all the boys' gangs have one feature in common: they engage in illegal or extralegal activities. Most of these activities are harmless: robbing orchards in the country, trespassing on empty buildings, trying to get into circuses or baseball parks without paying, smoking cigarettes made of corn silk, using dirty words and engaging in sexual experimentation, staying away from school and avoiding the truant officer (a municipal official whose job it is to see that children are at school when they should be, and who can have complaints made to the parents if they are not), cheeking policemen, and the like. What is important about these activities is that they are not only tolerated but expected and praised by the adults, especially the fathers; the successful flouting of authority is a sign of independence, of growing manliness; a boy who never attempted to do so would show grave signs of turning into a sissy. One more lesson is given in the proper attitude for an American to take toward authority and the law.

The line between tolerated, venial illegalities and those which should be regarded seriously is so finely drawn that it is understandable that many youngsters overstep the mark. If it is laudable to take apples off other people's trees, why not off other people's barrows? If it is manly to make and smoke cigarettes made of corn silk, why not ones made of marijuana? Most children, and most gangs, do learn without committing serious harm; but when children come from neighborhoods where the law is regarded overlightly, where the concentration of immigrants is high, from the slum borders where black and white and Asiatic mingle, where Jewish-gentile strife is severe among the adults, they can and do commit really serious crimes: desecrate churchyards and synagogues, commit grievous assaults and robberies, engage in a smaller way in the type of gang activities which has made the word notorious wherever American films or detective stories have an audience. It is not uncommon for white teachers in Negro schools to be attacked with knives; and cases have occurred of young boys shooting and killing their teachers.

Only a tiny minority of American children and youths engage in such criminal activity, but there is a fear, albeit almost unformulated, on the part of the adult community that the young will carry their defiance of authority too far, beyond the necessity of independent manliness. Serious community efforts are made to channel these energies and activities into such socially approved institutions as the Boy Scouts, Sea Scouts, and Camp Fire Girls; but though these have taken on typically American forms, with enormous emphasis on the competition for badges, they still smack too much of authority and regulation to be altogether congenial to most young Americans.

Society has, however, found a far more effective way for channeling youthful energy into socially acceptable channels, and one which is thoroughly congruent with the major emphases, with the constant pushing toward adulthood, and with the belief in the superior moral nature of womanhood. Any boy or girl who is not a roughneck (the term for those who carry their independence and uncouthness too far) or a sissy will try to be as attractive as possible to the opposite sex, will engage in the patterned precourtship, heterosexual behavior called "dating." The formal beginning of this type of behavior is quite often the commencement dance at the end of the sixth grade of school, that is to say in the child's twelfth summer. Some may start earlier, particularly in the South, and some later; but for the greater number this is the formal occasion for their entry into this preadult world. For this dance the children usually are given their first formal party clothes, for the girls long organdie dresses with short sleeves and full skirts, for the boys white trousers and double-breasted dark coats (the fashions may have already changed). Each boy must invite one of his feminine classmates to accompany him, and happy is the mother whose daughter receives many early invitations. This is the final stretch of the competition in which the parents have vicariously engaged since they compared the babies' weights in the hospital; if one's schoolgirl daughter is in constant demand, is popular, then she has been as well-equipped as is possible, one has been a success as a mother; if she spends too many nights of the week alone, above all if she is forced to spend Saturday nights at home, or with another unfortunate girl, that child has been a failure, and one had perhaps better concentrate on her education, so that her brains may give her the chance that her beauty and personality have failed to provide.

The mother cannot participate so directly in her son's successes, and the father is often somewhat ambivalent, feeling himself pushed aside by the rising generation, grudging the constantly increasing demands for money which numerous dates necessitate, disputing who shall have the evening use of the family car ("Gee, a girl won't look at you if you haven't got a car"). But though he may not participate so directly in the social triumphs of his son as the mother does in those of her daughter, yet he would be even more mortified if his son spent most of his evenings at home, or with other boys similarly unenterprising; for this would be proof that he had been a complete failure as an American father: he would have produced a sissy.

[h] Television has done, and is doing, for President Kennedy all that radio did for President Roosevelt.

IV

LOVE AND FRIENDSHIP

IN CHAPTER III, I have viewed the continuous competition between American children of the same age predominantly as it is seen and felt by the parents, and have taken relatively little account of the children's personal involvement. But of course the children are involved in it, most deeply and emotionally involved. For the parents the child's relative success gives the answer to the question: "Have I been a good American parent? Have I produced and equipped a child who can hold his own, make good, amount to something, reach heights which I cannot?" But to the child (and so to the adult) its own success means much more than that. "Am I successful?" comes to mean "Am I loved?" For from the very beginning, the mother's unqualified love and approval have been given to her child in proportion to its success. By adolescence most Americans have inextricably confused the two ideas: to be successful is to be loved, to be loved is to be successful. This confusion is even given a quasi-theological sanction, derived from the puritanism of New England as diffused by the schoolteachers: worldly success is an outward and visible sign of the love of God, of Providence; to be a failure signifies that one is unloved by God, that one has sinned, or, at the least, has not tried hard enough.

To gain one's mother's love, the prototype of all future love, it is not necessary that one should show love in return; one is loved for one's accomplishments vis-à-vis one's age mates, not in the first place for one's attitude and behavior toward one's mother. Love in America therefore tends to have a nonreciprocal quality: to be loved it is not necessary to love in return, but rather to be worthy of love. This of course does not mean that mutual love is absent in America, nor even rarer than in other countries, but there is superadded this nonsymmetrical component, which can only become symmetrical by identification, by conceiving the loved one to be, as it were, part of oneself, as worthy of love as oneself.

Because the child is pushed to the very limits of its capacity, because the conditions for its success are often so vague, or so far outside its control, the child becomes insatiable for the signs of love, reassuring it that it is worthy of love, and therefore a success. Now, the least of these signs of love is the attention of other people (in the first place the parents) or, at the minimum, their presence, so that their attention, if not immediately fixed on one, may be momentarily so directed. If nobody is there, if one is alone, how can one still the gnawing doubts that maybe one is not a success, not lovable, not worthy of love?

It is these feelings which make loneliness intolerable to well-adjusted Americans, and account for the numerous social features which are designed to obviate it: the absence of doors in all but the most private parts of most houses, the wedged-open doors of offices and studies, the shared bedrooms in colleges and boarding houses, the innumerable clubs and fraternal and patriotic associations, professional organizations, and conventions, the club cars on trains, the numberless opportunities and facilities given for casual conversation, the radio piped into every hotel bedroom,[i] into many railway cars and automobiles, left on incessantly in the house (for even the voice of the radio is better than silence). "I should go mad if I had to spend a week [or shorter period] alone" is a constantly reiterated remark which conceals real psychological truth under its surface exaggerations. Americans, psychiatrists as well as laymen, consider that there is something odd, something suspect, in a young person who deliberately eschews company and chooses privacy or loneliness. When they are judging Americans they are probably right, and such withdrawal is likely to be a schizophrenic symptom; but such standards cannot profitably be applied to people of a different upbringing, a different character.

The presence, the attention, the admiration of other people thus becomes for Americans a necessary component to their self-esteem, demanded with a feeling of far greater psychological urgency than is usual in other countries. This gives a special tone to the social relationships of Americans with their fellows (with the exception, on occasion, of marital and parental relationships): they are, in the first instance, devices by which a person's self-esteem is maintained and enhanced. They can be considered exploitative, but this exploitation is nearly always mutual: "I will assure you that you are a success if you will assure me that I am" might be the unspoken contract under which two people begin a mutual relationship. The most satisfying form of this assurance is not given by direct flattery or commendation (this by itself is suspect as a device to exploit the other) but by love, or at least the concentrated, exclusive attention which shows that one is worthy of interest and esteem.

It is only against this psychological background that what is probably the most singular feature of American social life can be understood: the "dating" which occupies so much of nearly every American's leisure time from before adolescence until betrothal, and which for many continues even after, if separation or satiety lessens the satisfactions to be derived from the betrothed, or if excessive individual anxiety demands more reassurance than betrothed or spouse or lover can give. "Dating" is idiosyncratic in many ways, but especially so in that it uses the language and gestures of courtship and love-making, without necessarily implying the reality of either. The overt differences of behavior which distinguish "dating" from courtship are so slight as to be barely perceptible; yet only in rare cases, and those involving unbalanced people, does confusion result—when both partners are American. "Dating" is a highly patterned activity or group of activities, comparable in some ways to a formal dance, in others to a very complicated competitive game; it is comparable to a dance in that the gestures employed do not have the significance they would have in other settings (witness the bows and curtsies of the minuet, the close embrace of the waltz and later ballroom dances); but it is more nearly comparable to such a competitive game as chess, in which the rules are known to, and observed by, both parties, but in which each move, after the opening gambit, is a response to the previous move of the other player. As in dances and games, the activity is felt to be enjoyable and rewarding for its own sake, and the more enjoyable the more nearly the partners or players are matched in skill and other necessary qualifications. The comparison with competitive games, such as chess, can be carried further; both partners must play with concentration and serious-ness, using all their ingenuity, within the accepted rules, to be the victor; apart from the pleasure of the game, there is also the pleasant enhancement to one's self-esteem that winning the game provides. There is one aspect, however, in which the comparison of "dating" to chess breaks down; in a successful date there should not be a loser; both parties should feel their self-esteem, their assurance, enhanced.

As far as I know, no other society has been recorded which has developed a similar institutionalized type of be-havior for its young people. A number of societies, of which the Samoans and the Trobrianders are well-known examples, allow for a period of sexual license and experi-ment before betrothal and marriage; but these are, and are meant to be, years of sensual and sexual satisfaction, sought for their own sake. In American "dating" sensual and sexual satisfactions may play a part (though this is by no means necessary) as counters in the game, but they are not the object of the exercise; the object of the exercise is enhanced self-esteem, assurance that one is lovable, and therefore a success.

A further complication arises from the fact that the words and gestures of love are regularly employed in "dat-

ing" without either party taking them for anything but
counterfeit, moves in the game; and yet Americans believe
very deeply and passionately in love (a concept not shared
by the Samoans, nor the Trobrianders, nor many of the
peoples of whom we have adequate studies). It is difficult
to find comparisons for thus using frivolously in one context words and gestures which may be of the greatest importance in another. A very far-fetched one could be
derived from the game of chess. In a period of monarchical
passions and court intrigue "Your queen is captured" or
"Your king is threatened" could have completely different
significance according to the settings in which the phrases
were used.

There is, finally, the complication that "dating,"
employing and being known to employ the words and
gestures of love-making, is admitted and abetted by
parents and teachers who, many of them, hold the puritan
attitudes toward sex and the pleasures of the body, even
though these attitudes do not seem to be held by most of
the younger generation.

Because "dating" is so idiosyncratic to Americans
(though the generality of Americans do not suspect this,
believing, like the rest of the world, that the behavior they
are used to is "human nature") and because it employs the
form—but not the content—of love-making, it has been
the cause of innumerable and serious misunderstandings
whenever young Americans have come in contact with
foreigners of the opposite sex. An invitation to a "date"
—a pleasant and mutually profitable evening to enhance
each other's self-esteem and demonstrate one's skill in the

game—is almost always interpreted by a non-American as an attempt at seduction; if it is indignantly repudiated, both parties are left angry and dissatisfied: if it is immediately acceded to, the American, at least, feels defrauded, as if one had set out for a hunt and the fox had insisted on sitting down in one's back yard.

In a "date" the opening move, at least overtly, should come from the boy, in the form of an invitation to the girl to spend the evening in his company. The basis of selection is somewhat different for the boy and for the girl. For the girl the object is to have as many invitations as possible, so that she can choose among them the partner whom she thinks can give her the best time, or who will be the most fun to compete with; for the boy the object is to have as his partner the girl who is most admired and most sought after by his companions and fellow rivals. A girl who only got a single invitation to an important social event (say a commencement dance), even though it was from the most desirable boy, the captain of the football team, would be doubtfully pleased (this, of course, on condition that they are not courting); a boy whose invitation is accepted by the local "belle" in similar circumstances has already gained a major social triumph. Consequently, participation in the "dating" pattern is somewhat different for the two sexes: all boys can and should take part in it, the level to which they aspire being dependent on their qualifications; but only the most successful and popular girls in each set do so fully, the rest having to be content with a steady boy friend, or even the companionship of a fellow unfortunate.

Unless an American boy is very poor, very maladjusted, or for some reason almost totally excluded from social life, "dating" and earning money for "dates" will occupy the greater part of his leisure time from early adolescence until betrothal. The social pressure toward doing so is very great. Thus in a typical Midwestern college fraternity the senior members insisted that the juniors have at least three "dates" a week; and further that these "dates" should be with girls who did honor to the fraternity, and, barring betrothal, should not be too frequently with the same girl. Such open control and supervision is unusual, but few Americans would quarrel with the standard of behavior demanded.

The experience of girls is much less uniform, since they are dependent on the boys' invitations, and the boys will invite the most popular girls obtainable. As a consequence some girls will have almost all their time taken up by "dates," while others have at most an occasional one, and many others drop out of the competition altogether until betrothal. The picture is clearest in formal dances.[j] The hostess attempts to have at least three men for every two girls, so that at any moment at least a third of the men are in the "stag line," whereas all the girls are dancing. A man from the stag line "cuts in on" a dancing couple by tapping the man on the shoulder and taking his place. By etiquette one cannot refuse to be cut in on, nor can one cut in on one's immediate successor; a third man must intervene before one can resume one's partner and conversation. A man should not abandon his partner until cut in on; and one of the greatest humiliations a girl can bear is not to be cut in on before her partner is satiated with her company. Such an unfortunate girl is not likely to be invited again, nor, if invited, to accept.

For many girls, consequently, the "dating" period is one of humiliation, of frustration, of failure. But though it is painful, it is not usually psychologically crippling. Such unsuccessful girls are often betrothed and married earlier and better than the "belles" who, many of them, find it difficult to give up such prebetrothal triumphs: and moreover a "belle" is rated by the amount of money spent on her, among other things, and the standard is too high for most young men to maintain regularly.

The "date" starts as an invitation from a young man to a girl for an evening's [1] public entertainment, typically at his expense, though since the depression girls occasionally pay their share. The entertainment offered depends on the young man's means and aspirations, and the locality; but it is in a public place always, and nearly always includes eating food together, the food being anything from an ice-cream soda at the local drugstore to the most elaborate and expensive meal that the locality can provide. Besides the food, the most usual entertainment is dancing—the place of the dance ranging anywhere from the cheap roadside café with a jukebox to the most expensive cabaret or country club. The male (the "escort") should call for the girl in a car (unless he be particularly young or poor) and should take her back in the car. If the entertainment proposed is of a formal or expensive nature, the man should

[1] There are a few "dates" which start in the afternoon watching athletic contests.

provide a corsage—flowers for the girl to wear on her dress or in her hair.

The corsage is the first sign of the man's estimate of his partner for the evening, partly through the expense of the flowers, and partly according to the extent to which they are particularly suited to the girl's appearance, personality, or costume. Every item of the subsequent entertainment gives further signs; the relative amount of money spent is important for the girl's self-esteem, and not in itself.

"Showing the girl a good time" is the essential background for a "date," but it is not its object, as far as the man is concerned; its object is to get the girl to prove that he is worthy of love, and therefore a success. In some cases superior efficiency in dancing will elicit the necessary signs of approval; but typically, and not unexpectedly, they are elicited by talk. Once again, the importance of words is paramount.

Since, on first "dates" the pair are normally comparative strangers to one another, a certain amount of autobiography is necessary in the hopes of establishing some common interest or experience, at the least to prove that one is worthy of the other's attention. These autobiographies, however, differ at most in emphasis, in tone of voice, from those which should accompany any American meeting between strangers. What distinguishes the "date" from other conversation is a mixture of persiflage, flattery, wit and love-making which was formerly called a "line" but which each generation dubs with a new name.

The "line" is an individual variation of a commonly accepted pattern which is considered to be representative of a facet of a man's personality.[2] Most men are articulately self-conscious about their "lines" and can describe them with ease; they are constantly practiced and improved with ever differing partners. The object of the "line" is to entertain, amuse, and captivate the girl, but there is no deep emotional involvement; it is a game of skill.

The girl's skill consists in parrying the "line" without discouraging her partner or becoming emotionally involved herself. To the extent that she falls for the "line" she is a loser in this intricate game; but if she discourages her partner so much that he does not request a subsequent "date" in the near future she is equally a loser. To remain the winner, she must make the nicest discriminations between yielding and rigidity.

The man scores to the extent that he is able to get more favors from the girl than his rivals, real or supposed, would be able to do. The proving time is the return journey from the place of public entertainment to the girl's home. A good-night kiss is almost the minimum repayment for an evening's entertainment; but how much more depends on the enterprise of the man, the self-assurance of the woman,

[2].The following extract from a provincial paper, *Capper's Farmer,* quoted in the *New Yorker* of December 14, 1946, illustrates the schoolboy style and development of a "line":

Special features are what make a line your own. Here's one—nickname friends for famous people. Call girl friends Hedy or Lauren and watch them preen. Fellows get a kick out of being referred to as Superman or Hope.

Twist your own double talk. Originate superlatives and expletives for your own use. Something a duller character would call "swell" might be "geegosh-gorgeous" to you. Let off steam by exclaiming the name of some plant such as, "Oh, heliotrope!" or "Oh, for the love of my Aunt Prunella!"

and the number of "dates" the pair have had together. This love-making is still emotionally uninvolved; it is still part of the game, though the gestures and intimacies and language are identical with true love-making; it is not, save most rarely, an attempt at seduction; and the satisfactions sought are not, in the first instance, sensual but self-regarding. The man should demonstrate his enterprise and prove that he is worthy to be loved by pressing for ever further favors; but the girl who yields too much, or too easily, may well be a disappointment, in exactly the same way as too easy a victory in tennis or chess may be a disappointment.

It is usual—but not essential—that intimacies should increase with each successive "date" with the same partner, up to the threshold of, but seldom including, actual intercourse. The contest continues in these later phases, though slightly less articulately; the victor is the one who makes the other lose self-control without losing it him (or her) self.

It must be repeated that the goal of "dating" is not in the first place sexual satisfaction. An "easy lay" is not a good "date," and conversely. Apart from professional or semiprofessional prostitutes, there are in most groups girls who create for themselves an illusion of popularity by promiscuity. Their telephone numbers may get bandied about, but they are not the girls who get the orchid corsages, or get taken to the ringside tables at the best restaurants. It would be a paradox, but not too great a one, to say that the converse was more nearly true: that the ideal date is one in which both partners are so popular, so skilled, and so self-assured that the result is a draw.

Although "dating" is a game for two players only, it is very often elaborated into a "double date" by two couples going to the same places together. Noteworthy in this is the fact that the deeper emotional bond is between the two friends of the same sex (usually, but by no means always, the men) who arranged the "double date." A still further elaboration is the "blind date," in which the couple have not met at all before the start of the evening's entertainment; this can occur through one partner of an arranged "date" asking the other to provide a companion for his (or her) friend, or through a visitor in a strange town calling up a girl whose number he has been given. This last situation was revealingly exploited over the commercial radio in 1943 and later in a program called "Blind Date." Pairs of young service men, chosen from the audience, had to compete over the telephone for the favors of invisible models, the model making her choice on the basis of a couple of minutes' telephone conversation, herself saying just enough to keep the conversation going. The winners spent an evening together at the Stork Club at the sponsors' expense; they were provided with corsages to give their partners and a little cash. The exhibitionist fervor with which the competitors put over their "lines," with a considerable part of the United States listening in, was extremely revealing.

"Dates" are public. The greater part of them, as has already been said, take place in public places; and even if there is not a witness for the final portion, as there is in "double dates," there is little expectation that what transpires will be secret. Though distorted by a certain amount of boasting, detailed accounts of past dates are among the most popular subjects of conversation with people of one's own sex and generation. As with the child recounting his triumphs in the play group or at school, it is a proper method of gaining other people's respect and admiration.

"Dating" is normally ended by betrothal, which is the almost inevitable sequel of a boy's concentration on one girl. "Dating" is almost by definition promiscuous; and America offers no pattern for prolonged concentration on a single partner for the young outside courtship and marriage—there is no analogue, for example, to the French student's *petite amie*. With the increase in emotional maturity, most young men feel the lack of content in the "dating" pattern as it is normally practiced; a few—the "wolves"—develop it into regular seductions; but for the majority it is succeeded by betrothal and marriage.

The majority of Americans marry young, in many cases directly after graduation from high school or college. Thornton Wilder in *Our Town* makes the stage manager say: "It's July 7th, just after high-school commencement. That's the time most of our young people jump up and get married. Soon as they've passed their last examinations in solid geometry and Cicero's Orations, looks like they suddenly feel themselves fit to be married." Mr. Wilder's play was set in a small New England town in 1904, and he made the marriage age somewhat over early for contemporary urban conditions; but Americans do still marry very early.

Such early marriage is due, in great part, to the fact that, with insignificant exceptions, American life gives no possibility for a liaison which would provide more than the uncomfortable intimacies in the back of an automobile for young people outside marriage; and, added to the natural urge of the gonads, there is a widely spread and deeply held belief that regular sexual intercourse is necessary for health, and that abstinence is as damaging as constipation.

Although nowadays many Americans reach marriage no longer technical virgins, the premarital experience of most has been confined to brief, and generally alcoholic, encounters in the backs of cars or temporarily deserted living rooms, with little comfort or ease and with uncertain privacy; and consequently marriage is for most Americans a legally sanctioned analogue to a first liaison. Although prostitutes exist in considerable numbers, their clients come predominantly from older men, typically from married men temporarily separated from their wives or from foreign-speaking immigrants. Brothels, formerly common and cheap enough, are now increasingly rare and expensive, and do not form a part of the education of most young Americans, as they do for most young Frenchmen or Italians.

Since marriages are contracted so early, and with so little experience to inform the choice made, it is not surprising that divorce is much commoner in America than in any other country. As the liaison was given official sanction, so must its ending receive it. Despite the fictions inherited from English and ecclesiastical law, divorce is fundamentally by consent, even though the laws governing it vary enormously from state to state. In many states the woman is outrageously favored as regards property settlements.

Divorce is normally followed almost immediately by re-marriage. The hygienic reasons which made the first marriage desirable are still operative; except among the rich in big cities and among the bohemian fringe there is no esteemed social role for the unmarried mature individual; and marriage, if nothing else, is the best protection against the terror of loneliness.

Marriage is meant to be founded on romance, on love, without any other considerations being involved. There are normally no financial transactions: the bride is not expected to bring a dowry nor the groom to make a marriage settlement. The parents of the married couple have no recognized financial obligations beyond the undefined assistance involved in "giving the young people a start."

Because the ecstatic phase of love is rarely long lasting, even though it be the sole reason for marriage, and is usually succeeded by domestic irritations and difficulties and the responsibilities of rearing a family, a very great value is placed by Americans on the period between adolescence and, say, the birth of the first child. By almost everybody this is considered the peak of life, after which there is a gradual but continuous decline. This period, roughly from twelve to twenty-five,[3] is Youth—the Best Years of Our Lives—and is almost without exaggeration the chief *raison d'être* of living; one of the major duties of

---

[3] Even ten years ago Youth would probably have been more fittingly described as the period between the ages of sixteen and twenty-five; but the constant pressure toward independence and maturity has now brought early adolescents into this category. The younger members of the group have special terms to describe them—"bobby-soxers" and "junior misses" for the girls being the best known.

those who have passed this period is to make certain that their successors can enjoy it at least as much as they did. One of the reasons why so much guilt was obscurely felt by older people for the depression which started in 1929 was that it marred the Youth of a whole generation; and one of the chief reasons advanced against sending American "boys" overseas before America entered the war, and for bringing them back as soon as possible after military victory, was that otherwise the irreplaceable years of their Youth would be frittered away. This emphasis on Youth is overwhelming in American popular entertainment, in films, in magazine stories and novels, in advertisements, and so on. In point of fact, Americans have nearly the greatest expectation of life of any peoples in the world and, like other urban societies, an ever-increasing number of old people in the population. But no medium of mass communication would enable one to learn this; Americans wish to think of themselves, to be presented as they were when they were at the peak of their life; they identify with their children rather than with their parents. By the same reasoning, Americans constantly refer to themselves as a "young nation." On many counts they could be considered the "oldest" nation, for no other major power is living under an eighteenth-century constitution, and few are more politically conservative; but Youth is so pre-eminently desirable that it is inevitably ascribed to the nation as a whole. By similar reasoning, the young conscripted soldier, the G. I., was felt and stated to be a "typical" representative of America, in a way that the older officers, or the peacetime clubwomen, are not and cannot be. Older

Americans, particularly the men, are nostalgic for their Youth; the emotion given to the phrase "Our Boys" (not Men, be it noted) as a description of conscripted soldiers by middle-aged male politicians differs in quality and intensity to that given by any other nation to its representatives in the forces. It is probable, though not as far as I know consciously formulated, that the relatively very large gratuities (bonuses) given to members of the forces (even though their whole time therein may have been spent behind a desk at home) are attempts to compensate for the irreparable loss of some years of Youth. Apart from the natural physical vigor, the two chief characteristics of American youth are the relative lack of responsibility and "dating." Objectively, "dating" is a particular kind of patterned precourtship behavior peculiar to the inhabitants of the United States; subjectively it is the most important and enjoyable occupation of the peak period of one's life, in retrospect acquiring ever-increasing charms surpassing both present and past reality, so that many attempts are made to provide a simulacrum for those whose years have removed them from the reality. It is hardly an exaggeration to say that for many Americans the "pursuit of happiness," described in the Declaration of Independence as an unalienable right, is an elegant periphrasis for "dating."

"Dating" is as important in the relations between young men as it is between young men and young women, or very nearly so. Some mention has already been made of the role which competition and rivalry with one's age mates play both in the choice of the "date" and in the scoring during its course. For the young man it can be said that the background presence of other males is a necessary ingredient for a successful "date." This is quite undisguised in the choice: a girl is desirable as a "date" in direct proportion to her popularity, that is to the extent that she is known to be considered desirable by other males. In the course of the "date" it is shown by the fact that success is counted by gaining more favors than one's rivals; merely to get the same is inadequate satisfaction, which helps account for the relative unpopularity—for "dating"—of the "easy lay." Moreover the triumphs of the "date" are doubly savored—in some cases only reach their full significance—in subsequent descriptions to one's fellows and rivals, in the men's "bull sessions" and their feminine equivalents.

Emotionally still more important is the pattern of "double dating." It is the proper and expected leisure-time behavior of friends. The greater the friends, the more the behavior is desirable, nay imperative.

The expected attitude between boys and young men of an age is one of friendly rivalry; they are the people against whom one must measure oneself in the first place, whose absolute success would be damaging, but whose relative success is a spur to further effort. Since equals or near equals all stand in the same relation to one another, the relationship is generally symmetrical and without intensity, on the surface pleasantly friendly, such aggression as there is showing itself in humorous comment and mockery of any slight personal eccentricity or characteristic, typically by means of the nickname or the "wise crack," a type of mordant criticism in which the potentially wounding character is covered by the wit of the phrasing.

Although this friendly jocularity covering the essential competition—so diffuse that it can embrace anybody one can recognize and remember—is the norm between the majority of males, it is expected that, at least up to courtship and marriage, there will be further relationships in which the rivalry is muted and the warmth of feeling increased. Typically, there is only one such relationship for each man at one time, though the relationship is not expected to be lasting; and in peacetime this relationship is typified by the "roommate"—two young men sharing the same bedroom, whether at college or in a town away from the parental homes.

This roommate or "buddy" relationship can be of any degree of warmth or intensity; but the greater the warmth and intensity, the more essential is it that the pair shall engage in "double dating"; at its most intense they may even make a play for the same girl, preserving their relationship by sharing her favors. This relationship has been admirably portrayed in the "Flagg and Quirt" series of plays and films, and has many parallels in real life. It is felt to be particularly virile.

It is considered essential that the warmer the relationship is between friends, the more ardently shall they pursue women together, because of the American panic fear of homosexuality. Among the generality of Americans homosexuality is regarded not with distaste, disgust, or abhorrence but with panic; it is seen as an immediate and personal threat.

The chief reason for this would seem to be the feminine conscience, the encapsulated mother, to which reference has frequently been made. Because every American man has a feminine component in his personality, there is always a deeply hidden doubt concerning his own masculinity; and any person or situation which might bring this into question is seen as a drastic threat to a man's integrity and reacted to with violence and panic. A second reason may well be that the constant pushing toward initiative and precociousness, up to and beyond the limit of strength, which is so marked a feature of American childhood, makes passivity an ever-present and ever-dangerous temptation. A third reason is undoubtedly the deep ambivalence which most American men feel toward women, as an inevitable result of their upbringing. Women are in childhood not only the main source of love and rewards; they are also the main source of punishment and threats of punishment, so that with most children love and hate, reliance and fear, become inextricably tangled. Since the negative components of this complex of attitudes may not be openly manifested without both public and personal disapproval, the positive components are constantly over-emphasized to hide from the rest of the world—but above all from oneself—the feelings which no proper man ought to have.

The complex of attitudes was most clearly demonstrated during the war. Alone among the warring nations, America automatically rejected from the armed services all recognizable overt homosexuals; indeed almost the chief object of the psychiatric interview at induction was an attempt to segregate these. It was frequently stated that

the easiest way to escape induction was to shave one's arm-
pits and use a strong perfume before the medical examination; nothing more was necessary. This selection was not
made through any belief that the homosexuals would be
less efficient soldiers; it was a necessary protection for the
rest. Even when there was a real shortage of manpower
there was no suggestion that these rejects should be re-
classified.

In America, as opposed to Western Europe, the homosexual is a threat, not to the young and immature, but
above all to the mature male; nobody is sure that he might
not succumb. This is particularly apparent in the numerous sketches and jokes on the subject which are current in
metropolitan theaters and burlesques; the humor is derived, not from the effeminate gestures and manner of
speaking of the homosexual, but from the situation in
which the comedian interprets the innocent activities of
his associate as an attack on his person.

Because of the belief that everybody is vulnerable in
this regard, because nobody is sure that he is not a sissy,
all possible precautions were taken to protect the conscripted soldier. The weeding out of open focuses of in-
fection was the first phase, but this was not considered
sufficient; for after all the inhabitants of the barracks were
all male. To maintain their heterosexual interests, the
soldiers were encouraged by the War Department, itself
enthusiastically seconded by the press and the public, to
cover the walls with pictures of scantily dressed girls on
which their eyes could rest last thing at night and first
thing in the morning; their morale was "built up" by frequent visits of attractive women entertainers to the camps;

every effort was made by the Red Cross, the U. S. O., the Stage Door Canteen, and similar organizations to provide female companionship (under supervision) during their hours off camp, until it would seem to a foreigner that the whole army would be in a state of exacerbated erethism. These activities were viewed with approval by the whole community; even the most puritanical groups apparently considered it normal and desirable. Many protests were made against making beer easily available to young recruits, but none, as far as I know, about surrounding them with semipornographic art work.

Under normal circumstances, all relationships between American males are colored by this panic fear of their own potential homosexuality. It is to demonstrate to themselves that this fear is groundless that they must so insistently display their interest in women; and the warmer the relationship with another man, the more important is it for both that they shall keep prominently displayed their heterosexual interests. The "double date" proves that the friendship is a safe one.

In the front lines the potential danger of the relationship usually could not be kept down to a safe level by "double dates" or shared mistresses, and under such circumstances friendships developed great emotional intensity. Easily the most frequent precipitating cause of "shell shock," of "battle fatigue," was melancholia following the death of one's "buddy," one's "side-kick"—the synonyms are numerous. When both parties were unharmed, however, the relationship rarely survived the return to the United States. There it became dangerous.

The lives of most American men are bounded, and their interests drastically curtailed, by this constant necessity to prove to their fellows, and to themselves, that they are not sissies, not homosexuals. Any interest or pursuit which is identified as a feminine interest or pursuit becomes deeply suspect for a man. This covers most of the major and especially the minor arts—decoration and furniture, gardening and the like. Poetry and painting—interest perhaps even more than practice—are dangerous pursuits, whereas novel writing, music, and architecture are relatively safe. Indeed, all intellectual pursuits and interests are somewhat tainted; and when American intellectuals meet together, an enormous amount of time is wasted in proving boisterously to each other that they are just regular fellows. Incidentally, it is interesting to note that the converse criteria do not apply to women. Eyebrows are raised and tongues wagged concerning a male interior decorator; but a female efficiency expert is not thought to be doubtfully feminine.

It is difficult to exaggerate the prevalence and urgency of this unconscious fear. Nobody can ever be quite sure he is safe. It was presumably to dramatize this endless insecurity that Charles Jackson in *The Fall of Valor* [4] made his unfortunate protagonist a married man of forty with two children.

I think a connection can be traced between the preva-

---

[4] In 1948, this book was, to the best of my knowledge, the only novel dealing directly with male homosexuality. The situation has certainly changed since then; a bibliography of novels on this subject published in the United States in the last fifteen years would be extensive.

lence and urgency of such fears and tendencies, and the drinking to become intoxicated which is typical of many Americans. A small minority use alcoholic amnesia ("drawing a blank," "passing out") systematically to still their consciences over actions their sober selves would disapprove of; but more important, and more general, is the social drinking which licenses a considerable increase of physical contact between the drinkers, typified by rather maudlin singing with arms around one another's necks. The warm pleasure felt by the relaxation of everyday taboos gives high value to such evenings. The feeling of psychological inadequacy which drives the more unfortunate into chronic alcoholism probably springs in many cases from the same source.

It follows that the relationship between American men is normally of very low intensity. All Americans want to be popular with their fellows, but this popularity is easily obtained and demonstrated: little is needed beyond the use of first names, the joke and the slap on the back, the easy sharing of drink and hospitality, fluency in conversation. Nearly all Americans have a fear of rejection, and stigmatize people who don't easily give these overt signs of friendship as "high hat" "snooty" or "snobbish," attempting to reject before they are rejected; for to be rejected, even by an overformal and unsmiling servant, suggests that one may be a failure, may be unworthy of love. In contrast, people who are prodigal with such simple signs of friendship, particularly to their economic and social inferiors, are praised as "regular guys," as "truly democratic." As a description of character, "democratic" is generally used to signify that a person of high social or economic status acts in such a way that his or her inferiors are not reminded of their inferiority. There are no political connotations.

Because of their diffuseness and lack of intensity most American friendships between men are strictly contemporaneous. Nostalgia for lost Youth keeps some old relationships alive between people who have shared the same experiences,[5] but most Americans after marriage replace the friendly-competitive group of age mates by their present nearest rivals—their business or professional associates, and often their neighbors, the parents of their children's friends. Americans change both residence and job with the greatest of ease; and with each change of either, friends are changed, too. This does not mean that people are not conscious of preferences; but these are seldom important enough to be worth the effort of keeping alive when propinquity or common pursuits have disappeared. For many American men, sufficient friendships are found in the numerous service and patriotic clubs and associations—Rotary, Lions, Kiwanis, Elks, Free Masons, American Legion, and so on—which they join so frequently and with such enthusiasm.

This should not be taken to imply that Americans are

[5] The most striking of these revivals of the companionship of Youth are the class reunions which take place at universities. For a few days men leave their homes, their businesses, their wives, their children, and their grandchildren to live in college dormitories, and attempt to recapture their Youth by reminiscence softened with alcohol, by dressing up in peculiar costumes and by indulging in antics unsuitable to their years. In common speech a university is an *alma mater*, cherishing mother, and for a few days these middle-aged and elderly men attempt to get back from her their Youth.

friendless compared with Europeans; the converse would be more nearly true, except among the poorest of the floating population. But generally friendship has extension rather than depth, and is founded more on common interests than on congeniality of character. As nearly every Western European must have experienced in recent years, the American is remarkably ready to give and receive friendship. Like so much of the domestic equipment which Europeans envy, it is for them less a luxury than a necessity.

---

[1] Television and Muzak have added to the available distractions.
[2] This paragraph is no longer valid. See Postscript p. 259.

V

MAN A MACHINE?

THE SIGNS of friendship, of love, are a necessity for the American. He is insatiable in his demands for them, for any occasion on which they are witheld raises the gnawing doubt that maybe one is not lovable, not a success. There is no occasion, however trivial or however important, which brings two or more people together in which such signs are not desired. The smallest purchase should be accompanied by a smile and by the implied assurance that the vendor is delighted and privileged to serve you; the weightiest business or political conference must start with those greetings and anecdotes which demonstrate that the conferers like one another. There are no alternatives to these signs; unsmiling subservience produces discomfort, unsmiling arrogance, fear and hostility. The emotional egalitarianism of America demands that all relationships shall bear some resemblance to those of love and friendship.

One of the most paradoxical illustrations of this situation can be seen in the South, in the attitude demanded by the whites from the Negroes. The Negroes are kept in their subservient position by the ultimate sanctions of fear and force, and this is well known to whites and Negroes alike.

Nevertheless the whites demand that the Negroes shall appear smiling, eager, and friendly in all their dealings with them. Any impassivity or withdrawal—and how much more sullenness—is interpreted as impertinence or hostility; and any Negro who fails to demonstrate a friendliness which nobody could rationally expect him to feel is stigmatized as "uppity."

Custom and votes, other things being equal, go to the man who most adequately demonstrates friendly interest. In a pamphlet, *Political Primer for all Americans*, put out in 1944 by the Congress of Industrial Organizations to induce labor sympathizers to enter local politics, the center page is occupied by a double drawing entitled "The Politician—How He Grows." One picture shows a speaker on top of an imposing structure entitled "Public Office" seen from the front; the second shows the rear elevation with a ladder by which the speaker has reached his eminence. The rungs of the ladder are labeled, starting from the bottom, "Knowing the neighborhood—listening but not arguing—knowing names and places—ringing doorbells—doing odd jobs—working at headquarters—starting discussions—knowing the 'bosses'—speaking up at meetings —doing favors—resolving conflicts—getting votes." From the lowliest municipal official to the highest offices in the land, these rules, *mutatis mutandis*, are operative; and a memory for first names and personal hobbies is likely to secure more votes than the wisest legislation.

Because of their great commercial importance, the manifestations of these signs of friendship and love cannot be left to the hazard of temperaments to whom such behavior is congenial. They are taught and learned as part of the professional equipment of a great number of the people whose business it is to attract the custom of the public. Serious classes receive instruction in the Smile that Wins, the Handshake of Good Fellowship, Making the Visitor Welcome, Salesmanship as a Vocation, The Voice with the Smile. These manifestations are sometimes carried to very considerable lengths. Some resort municipalities and hotels have professional greeters who welcome new arrivals as if they were long-lost friends. As well as friendship, sexual interest is feigned: most airliners and other means of luxury travel have pretty "hostesses," [1] a considerable part of whose duty it is to go through the preliminaries of "dating" with any unattached male traveler; and in some drive-in cafés in the West and Southwest, coffee, coca cola, and hot dogs are brought to your car by beautiful young women so nearly naked that the undoing of a couple of knots would leave them completely bare. The knots of course never are undone during working hours, and few customers ever see again these inviting wenches after they have swallowed their snack; but the implicit suggestion adds relish to the food consumed, and may induce the customer to go a few miles out of his way to stop at the same place again, which is the whole object of such titillation.

At the other end of the scale, derelict diners made out of old railway carriages standing on waste lots at the entrance

---

[1] It is possible that "hostesses" were originally hired by airline companies to shame nervous male passengers: to show fear where a pretty girl seemed quite confident would brand one a "sissy."

to little towns try to attract customers by conspicuously displaying flyblown notices promising "Courteous Service," "You are Welcome." During the war, when there was a great demand for blood plasma, blood banks were set up in a great number of communities by the American Red Cross and were run with great efficiency; in many of them the last volunteer lady one met after one had given one's blood was the Thanker, stationed at the exit to thank warmly and graciously each donor as he left the building. This job was properly counted as important war work.

Historically this learned demonstration of the signs of friendship and love was probably exploitative on the part of employers, who noticed that salesmen and women to whose temperaments such behavior was congenial attracted more customers and made greater sales, and demanded similar behavior from all their employees. But today the situation has received a far greater extension. Women enroll themselves in "Charm Schools" and conscientiously follow the instructions which will provide them with charm; and for more than ten years Dale Carnegie's *How to Win Friends and Influence People* has been a consistent best-seller and its instructions have been most carefully followed. It teaches, with excellent and vivid detail, how to behave so that people will think you like them, how to *act* friendship. The question of sincerity does not arise; the reader is unquestionably sincere in his desire to achieve the aims promised in the title; his success is dependent on the conviction with which he follows the instructions.

What is important in this and the many other books and

schools which promise social success and happiness is the implicit view of the personality, of the self. For the Americans who buy the books and join the schools we are not "as God made us"; by taking thought we may not be able to add a cubit to our stature but we can change the figure we present to the world. The Personality is seen as something to be manipulated, almost as a raw material, Character as subordinate to Will.

Here, once again, the second generation is probably crucial. The children of foreigners from every land, with every type of temperament and every physical constitution, were turned into Americans at school; personality need not be merely the product of inherited characteristics and the impact of experience; it need not be a slow growth which must be fostered; it can also be manipulated and remolded nearer to the heart's desire, or at least to the type which will win friends and influence people, bring in the orders, put over a "commercial" smoothly, leave the customer contented.

The implications are many. The unsociable or eccentric person is to be blamed, not pitied (at least outside New England); he could change his personality if he wanted to and tried hard enough; the fact that he has not done so shows either a weak will or more probably "orneriness" and contempt for the opinions of others. "You, too, can be popular . . ."

Personality is, as it were, a raw material to be developed and exploited, in a manner analogous to any other raw material; the enterprising and fortunately circumstanced can develop and exploit it for their own benefit; but many will perforce sell or lease their charm, their frankness, their warmth, their sexual appeal, their voice, to an employer to exploit for his benefit in the same way as they will sell their labor. A winning smile or a pleasant voice is nearly as marketable a business commodity as a knowledge of accountancy or skill in mining. It is a curious comment on the change in values that "selling oneself" is a meritorious and praiseworthy act on the part of a young person setting out in life, and is a necessary preliminary to "selling" an idea or a project, and, in most cases, to acquiring a job. A person incapable of "selling" him or herself is badly handicapped.

To repeat, the personality is viewed as a commodity, a raw material: and like other raw materials it can be manipulated, transformed, studied. Many of the more recent developments of American psychology, both industrial and academic, have such a point of view concerning the personality among their underlying assumptions; and, in the accounts of theories and experiments, both specialized and popular, the number of metaphors and descriptions of human behavior drawn from machines is remarkable and consistent.[2]

The study and manipulation of the personality is the final development of an attitude which has been character-

[2] See for industrial psychology the work of Elton Mayo and much of the work done in the General Electric plants; for academic psychology the sociometry of Dr. Moreno, many of the developments of behaviorism, and much of the topological theory of the late Dr. Kurt Lewin. The mentioning of these works in this context should not be taken to imply a criticism of them.

istic of America during most of its independent existence, and which accounts in great part for its wealth and power. This is the careful analysis and consequent exploitation of human skills and physical movements. One of the two basic components in the development of America's technological genius has been the viewing of man as a working machine.

American technology developed with the industrial revolution; for obvious historical reasons the elaborate artistic crafts—for example, fine weaving, cabinetmaking, fine glass, goldsmith's work—which date from several centuries earlier and which were developed in a long tradition of apprenticeship, were never indigenous to the United States. As the demand for these fine products developed, Americans first of all imported the finished articles and subsequently the craftsmen who had learned their trades in Europe.[3] They then proceeded to analyze systematically the finished article, the implements used for making it, and the gestures which the skilled craftsmen employed; they questioned the necessity, the validity of each implement, of each gesture; and they then devised machines to do as much of the work as possible, and reduced the gestures to a series of controlled and analyzed movements which could often be learned in fewer hours than the original craftsmen took months to learn their skills. In some cases, of course, the final products had less individuality, less finish, fewer lasting qualities than the original craftsmen's creations; but they were produced in

[3] See Mead, *op. cit.*, Chapter XIII.

millions instead of hundreds, and so much less labor time was involved in their making that replacement ceased to be a problem.

This process is still continuing. It is well known that the greater number of scientists who made the development of the atomic bomb possible learned their craft in Europe, whatever their country of allegiance. Perhaps even more striking is the current development of rocket weapons, of the V-2; here the whole historical process was recapitulated. America started by acquiring the finished product, the German rocket, through capture, and analyzed that; then she imported the craftsmen, the German scientists, and analyzed their behavior; and then, when these analyses had been completed, she set about producing bigger and better rockets, capable of going higher and traveling farther than the German originals, and—one does not doubt, though as far as I know it has never been officially disclosed—able to be produced in enormous quantities.

Besides the analysis of skills, which has been part of the American attitude toward the world for the greater part of its independent history, there has been the analysis of the gestures and movements of workers, as parts of the machine process, which has been the distinguishing mark of American development in the twentieth century, and with which the names of Taylor, Ford, and Bedaux have been particularly connected. Mass production depended on three things: the invention of the endless band, the fragmentation of the manufacturing process, and the analysis of the gestures needed at each stage of the process to advance it to the next stage. This last was the most essential part; unless this was done the other components would have been ineffective, for it would have been impossible otherwise to have achieved and maintained the even speed which is an essential part of the assembly line.

For the worker this development has meant the consistent depreciation of specialized skill as a component of his value in the labor market. The complication of the engineers' profession has become increasingly greater; but the greatest number of jobs in modern mass manufacture can be learned in, at most, a few hours and perfected in a few weeks; and good physical co-ordination and stamina are often more valuable qualities than skill. The worker's emotional or intellectual connection with his job is minimized; housing and schools may keep him in one place [4] but not professional interests; Americans can and do change jobs with the greatest of ease and almost any motive is justifiable.

It is worth noting that the extremely slight emotional connection with one's job and, often, ignorance of the end-product are not consciously felt by Americans to be a deprivation. When the details of the manufacture of the atomic bomb were made public, most Europeans (I among them) and a few Americans with European values thought that the tens of thousands of workers engaged in work whose end-product nobody knew must have felt

[4] The mobility of urban Americans is normally extremely great. In 1937 a study was made by the Bell Telephone Company of Cleveland, Ohio, which revealed that less than 25 per cent of the city's inhabitants had lived in their present home for more than five years. Subsequent investigations have shown even more striking figures of continuous movement.

supremely demoralized, dispirited, and frustrated, almost as though they were engaged in forced prison labor. But this was not the case. Numerous conversations with former workers at Oak Ridge and the other atomic plants demonstrated that it was not felt to be different (except for the isolation) from any other job paying similar money for similar hours.

From the point of view of the engineer, the man is part of the machine, performing movements which no machine—so far—has been devised to do. This view is perforce accepted by the worker; he has no choice but to admit that his body can be used as an adjunct to a machine, that his muscular strength and co-ordination are raw materials to be exploited in the most efficient and economical way, that his work should consist in learning a few routines and repeating them endlessly. It would appear that this is not consciously felt to be humiliating or degrading by the majority of workers, but is rather accepted as a necessary condition of life; the monotony of the work is made tolerable by daydreaming; and more attention is directed to the conditions of work than to the fact that one's personality and skill are almost completely divorced from the occupation of so many working hours. But though such conditions are accepted, there is evidence to suggest that they are, perhaps unconsciously, felt to be unsatisfying; the very great mobility of unskilled American labor and the high turnover at most mass-production plants indicate a general feeling of restlessness and searching; and this mobility has as a secondary result an increase in the loneliness and isolation Americans dread so much.

This lack of involvement in one's job would seem to have two major psychological derivatives: a diminishing of concentration, and an increase in the avoidance of boredom outside one's job. These two aspects are really complementary: only a moron could, or would need to, concentrate deeply on the uniform repetition of an ordained series of movements; and so work hours are inevitably hours of boredom made tolerable by diffuse daydreaming. Though this boredom is not considered humiliating it is considered painful (as, earlier, physical fatigue was considered painful) and every effort is made to avoid its repetition outside working hours. Hence the entertainment industries which in America are constantly increasing in size, scope, and personnel employed; hence, too, it would seem, the great and increasing use of depressants, particularly alcohol, as a device for averting the threat of boredom.

Many Americans use their leisure for constructive activities—it is surprising how many Americans build their own houses—though these, too, are constantly being simplified till all that is needed is the careful following-out of detailed instructions; but for most the greatest recompense for being part of a machine in one's working hours is the mastery of a machine in one's leisure. Most American men handle machines with assurance, great competence and great joy; hours spent in pulling to bits and reassembling better a broken-down machine are a constant pleasure; and the nearest approach to ecstasy in many young men's lives came during the war when they were put in charge of giant bulldozers or the more powerful airplanes.

I think it can be said that, without adopting the values of any particular society, there is real psychological impoverishment inherent in this increasing lack of interest and involvement in the work which still occupies a considerable proportion of most men's waking hours. It is, however, fatally easy to exaggerate this, to be romantic about the pleasure and pride the craftsman got from the exercise of his skill and forget the squalor and poverty to which he so often returned when his work was done. But be it admitted that there is real psychological improverishment, possibly of a serious nature, involved in thus treating man as an adjunct of the machine; it is the price that Americans have had to pay, and have paid willingly, for their extraordinary technological development which has produced so much material wealth, measured by any possible standard, that, though the Americans only represent about 6½ per cent of the world's population, they own 20 per cent of the world's wealth. Despite the marked unevenness in distribution, the benefits of this wealth are shared by the greater part of the American population. In the words of Roosevelt's second inaugural address, a third of the population—above all the inhabitants of the southern states and the slum dwellers of the big cities—are "ill-fed, ill-clothed, ill-housed"; but the remaining two thirds enjoy a command of goods and services, of horsepower per man, of food and housing, of leisure and entertainment, which cannot be approached, much less paralleled, for a similar proportion of the population in any other society in the world. The "American standard of living" is no idle boast; the majority of the American population enjoys, by all material criteria, a way of life superior to that of all except a very small minority in the rest of the world. If poverty is conquered for humanity, if ease and plenty are put within the reach of all—surely a desirable aim—it will be thanks to America's technological inventiveness and example. It will not be without cost; indeed, for other societies, the cost will almost certainly be considerably greater; communism, which promises the same material goods for the future, demands the present surrender of far more important aspects of the independent personality.

If the analysis and the atomization of movement and gesture have been accompanied by such great rewards, the same cannot generally be said of the atomization of knowledge, which has been an almost uncalculated by-product of the same process. Just as gestures, movements, and machines have been split up into their smallest component parts, so has knowledge tended to be reduced to a series of disconnected and isolated facts, all comparable to one another as all dollar bills are comparable to one another; the more one has of either the better, and a learned man tends to be considered a sort of fact millionaire. The most obvious display of this attitude is given by the enormously popular quiz programs over the radio, headed by *Information Please*, in which America is invited to "stump the experts." What actually happens in this program is that the memory of the "experts" is tested for their retention of irrelevant and recondite facts; although there is occasional wit in the phrasing of the answers, no intelligence of any sort is involved, merely the recollection of abstruse quotations and snippets of history. In the other quiz programs the level of reconditeness and abstruseness is lowered, but it is memory rather than knowledge that is tested.[5]

This attitude toward knowledge is ingrained in the American educational system. From the intelligence tests given to preschool moppets, to the examination given before admission to postgraduate studies, candidates are rated to a very large extent by their retention of unrelated and un-co-ordinated facts and for verbal facility. A fairly typical examination paper consists of a check list—questions on one side of a paper and a series of alternative answers on the other, the candidate being required to mark the correct answer. This, of course, makes for ease of marking and for strict comparability between the achievements of different competitors and different groups of competitors. The printing of the incorrect answers on the papers almost inevitably reduces the significance of the correct answer to that of an isolated fact, despite the ingenuity with which, in some cases, questions are developed out of their predecessors. For the most part the relevance of these assorted gobbets of information to one another or to anything outside the examination is little developed.

In times of crisis, when there is a demand that a great many people shall suddenly acquire new skills, the atomization of knowledge pays rich dividends. During

[5] Apparently the chief satisfaction derived by the listener to these programs is the humiliation of the expert, the authority, by the ordinary man. See the article by Herta Herzog in *Radio Research* edited by Paul Lazarsfeld and Frank Stanton (New York, Duell, Sloan and Pearce 1941).

the war, when navigators, map makers, naval and aero-
nautical engineers, speakers of Japanese and Chinese, and
many other specialists were required in great numbers,
America was able to instill the skills into the requisite
numbers with astonishing speed. Young men who had
never seen the sea were fitted to take charge of destroyers
and submarines in a few months. They certainly lacked
the ease and assurance of men whose lives had been spent
in learning the one task, but they acquired the necessary
skill: they won their battles. By breaking down into its
component parts the requisite skill and knowledge, the
American authorities were able to impart the necessary
training at a speed which no other nation could approximate.

Apart from the ease with which new routines are
learned, there are few rewards for the atomization of
knowledge, and there are very considerable drawbacks. It
has already been remarked that most Americans feel no
conscious uneasiness in taking part in a manufacturing
process about which they know nothing, not even the end
product. Unfortunately too many feel the same lack of
uneasiness in taking part in a social process of whose work-
ings they know nothing, or next to nothing. For the worker
engaged in mass production intellectual passivity is inevitable. The greatest political danger to America is that
similar intellectual passivity toward their society should be
demonstrated by a large proportion of its citizens. Just as
American society and the American national character
differ profoundly from those of Europe, so do the probable
future political developments and risks. The probability

of communism in its European form being adopted in the United States is so slight that it is surprising that it can even be used as a bogey. The risk that European-style fascism will develop is hardly greater—if for no other reason than the typical American rejection of overt authority.[6] The great threat to American democracy lies in the apathy and passivity of its citizens; an increase in these qualities, and a further lowering of the caliber of Americans who make politics a career, might well lead to a virtual breakdown of the state; or alternatively this apathy may leave them open to the manipulations of a self-appointed elite of social engineers—to use a popular and extremely revealing phrase.

This apathy and passivity are almost certainly enhanced by the increasing atomization of knowledge, and even of communication. The type of communication to which most Americans are most constantly exposed is television; and television, as it has been developed in America, is increasingly atomic. Most non-Americans who have criticized the American radio have done so on the grounds of taste, finding esthetically unpleasant the commercial advertising which interrupts all except a minority of prestige broadcasts every five minutes or so. The esthetic arguments are possibly valid; but they would appear of secondary importance compared with the psychological effects. The constant switching of attention from the merits of a political program to the merits of a proprietary purgative, from the advance of an army to the advance in

---

[6] Racial discrimination, always present, may well become exacerbated; but racialism is not an integral part of fascism.

the sales of a dentifrice, from a talk on the application of science to agriculture to the claims of the "scientific" preparation of a breakfast cereal, from the discussion of foreign loans to the facilities of installment buying, from the development of the United Nations to the bargains of a department store, must have one of two effects on the listener: either the communication must be received in the smallest discrete gobbets, to avoid confusion, or all values must be transformed so that all the items purveyed are of equal interest and validity. The latter, of course, is the aim of the sponsors, and it seems probable that it is being increasingly achieved. In those numerous cases where commentator or chief speaker voices the commercials with, if anything, greater emphasis and appearance of conviction than he or she gives to the rest of his material the confusion is almost inevitable.

The atomic aspect of American T V is most striking in those programs whose noncommercial portions contain material of potential civic importance, but it is not confined to these. The most popular entertainment programs consist of a series of amusing non sequiturs uttered by a small group of stereotyped characters. The jokes are often excellent, and can easily be incorporated into conversation; but only in short portions of a few programs (notably Fred Allen's) is the order of the jokes meaningful. The greater number of scripts could be cut up and reassembled in any other order without losing comprehensibility or laughs. The one general type of entertainment program in which the continuity is important is the serial drama, the "soap opera," which occupies so much broadcasting time during the day; they require continuous attention, if a minimum of concentration. Like the films, the other major means of mass communication, they provide mass-produced fantasies to inform and supplement private daydreaming.

Although the atomic aspect of communication is most marked in the mass media, it is also a noticeable component of face-to-face conversation. The "wise crack" normally stands alone, self-sufficient and without context. A marked feature of the conversation of American men consists in the interchange of assorted facts, especially such as can be expressed in numbers, once the conversation has ceased to be personal. These pieces of information are normally not used to support an argument and not even necessarily as a disguised aid to boasting: the vital statistics and growth of a community, the size and productivity of a factory, the details of the performance of a machine, are frequently repeated for their own sake. Such repetition is friendly in intention, and even generous; if the listener happens to retain any portion of the facts imparted to him, he has thereby increased his fund of information.

This custom of looking at facts discretely, as though each were separate and each of equal validity, has important political repercussions. What members of other societies often consider to be the contradictions of American policies are quite honestly not so perceived by the Americans, because the different aspects are not considered to be connected. The most obvious instance is the frequent discrepancy between American political and economic demands or actions. For peoples whose way of looking at the world is—for want of a better word— holistic, the atomicism of the American view of the world is incomprehensible; and very often cynical and immoral intentions are imputed because the observers supply connections between different statements or acts of which the Americans were completely unconscious. In some ways the American view of the world is the furthest removed from that of many primitive tribes, from what can perhaps be called the primitive view of the world. Although there are some notable exceptions, most primitive peoples view the varied phenomena of the universe they know as deeply and intricately interconnected, so that actions in one sphere will influence or be influenced by actions in a completely different sphere—a view of the world typified by various systems of magic and taboo. In Western Europe many of these connections are rejected, but the universe is still conceived as composed of multiple and intricate interconnections. In America there is a growing tendency to regard each aspect of the universe separately and discretely, as though each existed independently of the other. The predominant American philosophy, pragmatism, is less a system of the universe than an attitude toward the universe.

The contrast between the European and the American view of the universe is dramatically and schematically illustrated by the type of analogies each group employs. In Europe—perhaps particularly in England—institutions and processes are continually being compared to trees: pruning and staking may guard against undesirable developments, proper care and attention will hasten the growth, neglect and bad treatment will retard, possibly kill it. Running through much of English thinking is this parallel with organic growth; whether they are dealing with the United Nations, the independence of dependent peoples, the development of character, or economics, they tend to think of them as though they had their own internal laws of growth and development which should be wisely fostered but cannot greatly be hurried or retarded. In similar situations Americans think of machines. A device has been made to produce a given result by combining a series of discrete parts. If it doesn't produce the desired result, or doesn't produce it quickly or efficiently enough, it is no use waiting for it to develop; one should scrap it, and then use the component parts, together with whatever additions may be necessary, to produce a device which will be effective. And even if it is reasonably efficient, that is no reason for sitting back and letting it alone; what was good enough for yesterday will not be good enough for tomorrow.

These attitudes can be applied only to institutions and processes which can be compared to machines. To the few for which the comparison is felt not to be apt—chiefly the institutions embodied in the Constitution of the United States and religions—such an attitude would be considered to approach blasphemy. This reserved and sacred area is a small one, and almost entirely confined to the United States; that aside, there is little inside America and practically nothing outside which would not be improved by being taken to pieces and remade to a more modern model.

VI

THE WORLD OF THINGS

I STATED in the last chapter that one of the two basic components in the development of America's technological genius is the viewing of man as a working machine: the other component is the revolutionary and masterful attitude which the American has toward materials, toward things. In his attitude toward the material world the American is and has long been a revolutionary: old traditions and ancient rules have been tested and, if found wanting, discarded without remorse. To any protest of the break with tradition, of the impracticality of a new proposal, the response has always been: "Why not?" The alleged boast of the Seabees, "The difficult we do at once, the impossible takes a little longer," might be the motto of nearly every American man faced with things.

Few contrasts are more marked than the attitudes of the American man toward things and toward people. In their dealings with other people, most American men (though not most American women) would appear to be troubled by a feeling of basic insecurity, which is inadequately disguised by the overcompensations of brashness and boasting; their insatiable need for reassurance has already been described. In contrast, their attitude toward things is untroubled by ambiguity, serene and confident, audacious and creative to an extent that no other society in the world has seen or imagined. In personal relations, the American woman is generally dominant, whether she be physically present or not; the world of things is the kingdom of the American man.

The American completely dominates his material. The search for its natural qualities and stresses, the cunning study of its nature and tendencies, which have been the distinguishing mark of the craftsman in most societies, have little place in the American approach to things. His vision, his plan, comes first; if nature does not provide the requisite materials, then he will do his utmost to improve and invent materials which will realize his vision.

It is probable that this attitude developed under frontier conditions. On the frontier—and indeed in the America of Thomas Jefferson's dreams—each family had to be nearly independent; mastery in a single skill could never keep an isolated family alive; competence, or at least adequacy, in a great number was essential for survival. A heavy premium was put on improvisation. Further, whether the frontiersman were immigrant or native born, he would almost certainly be confronted with a considerable number of novel raw materials, and the absence of those he was used to; for different portions of the continental United States vary considerably in their flora, their fauna, their minerals and their climate. This variation was much more marked a century ago, before most of the larger animals had been destroyed, before the Indians—themselves most various—had been exterminated or enclosed, before the country was laced with railways and roads which could distribute the resources of all areas. Moreover, these novel raw materials were generally present in great quantities; it is only in the last forty years that the notion of conservation has gained any wide currency. Plentiful though these strange raw materials were, will and energy were needed to acquire them, ingenuity and imagination to adapt them to the current needs. There was no time for careful experiment; survival itself often depended on immediate exploitation.

A sufficient number did survive to transmit their attitude to those who came after, to make it the dominant American attitude toward raw materials, toward things. It is an attitude which is not, as far as I know, shared by any other society. It can perhaps best be expressed negatively. It is completely opposite to the traditional attitude of peasants, for whom the land and its products are, as it were, part of themselves, of their ancestors and descendants, so that their histories and fortunes are conceived of as intertwined, so that there is at least a measure of identification between man and material. With the partial exception of the South, this complex of attitudes is completely alien to most Americans; there is no identification between man and his raw material; man is superior and apart, imposing his will on the inhuman universe.

These attitudes are seen most clearly in the case of land itself. Land is not something to be loved and succored, but something to be exploited. Significantly often, the terms of mining are applied to agriculture. Crops are extracted, land is mined—the vegetable world is constantly being spoken of, and treated, as though it were a mineral world. Crops are extracted from a piece of land until it is exhausted, after which the land is abandoned, in exactly the same way as metal is extracted from a vein until that is exhausted and the mine abandoned.

Of course this treatment of the land has had disastrous results in erosion and the creation of dust bowls—man-made deserts—and conservation has become imperative. But this has not deeply changed the attitude toward land. Instead of mines, farms and forest lands have come to be compared to factories, where the maintenance of the plant is necessary for the production of goods. Land is still a raw material, no more to be loved or identified with than a lump of iron or an oil well under the soil. Although in the technical sense nearly half the population of the United States is rural (living in towns of less than twenty-five hundred inhabitants) and nearly a quarter is engaged in the extractive industries of agriculture, fishing, and forestry, there is no American analogue to the European or Asiatic peasant. People may get their living from the land, but the culture, the values, and the diversions are today predominantly urban.

A partial exception should be made for people who get their living from animals—the herders, the cowboys, the trappers. It is impossible to regard animals as things, to treat them as minerals; and people who work with animals regard themselves, and are regarded by most of their fellow Americans, as exceptional and somehow romantic. They are a very small group.

For the vast majority of Americans the world of things

is a world of inanimate objects, of minerals, or of things which can be likened to minerals—land, wood, water. And in this world they are supreme, endlessly ingenious in transforming things to man's use and enjoyment and profit. This ingenuity in the exploitation of things has, fairly recently, been given a special term—"know-how"; it is rightly considered peculiarly American.

It should be noted that know-how is not identical with inventiveness. The number of basic inventions made by native-born Americans is surprisingly small; but once the basic invention is made, from railroads and automobiles to radar and penicillin, Americans are unsurpassed in their improvement, industrial adaptation, and above all diffusion. One of the chief illusions which Americans cherish about themselves, and which they have succeeded in imposing on much of the rest of the world, is that Americans are the originators of most of the basic modern inventions. There would appear to be a general feeling that, since America is, without question, the country with the greatest technical development, the basic inventions which made this technical development possible must have originated in America. This concept is developed by fairly consistent *suppresio veri* and *suggestio falsi*; the foreign origin of major inventions is passed over in silence, and American adaptations or even the first American model are celebrated with the greatest pomp and circumstance. Although outside the realm of invention, the myth that Lindbergh was the first man to fly the Atlantic is a typical example of such distortion of fact.

American technological genius shows itself much less in

invention than in improvement and diffusion. The folk recipe for making a fortune is revealing: "Make a better mousetrap, and the world will beat a path to your door." It is improvement, not novelty, which is recommended to the ambitious young man.

To improve the design and increase the supply of things adapted to man's use and enjoyment is the most important object of life. This object is pursued with a fervor and a sense of dedication which in other societies and at other times have been devoted to the search for holiness and wisdom, or to warfare. Any device or regulation which interferes, or can be conceived as interfering, with this supply of more and better things is resisted with unreasoning horror, as the religious resist blasphemy, or the warlike pacifism. It is this feeling which keeps popular support behind the antitrust laws, which makes the alleged slaughter of little pigs in the early days of the New Deal so much more potent a subject of recrimination than any of the other novel activities then undertaken, which evokes a general and genuine admiration and feeling of personal participation in figures of production, in records broken, in the creation of the bigger and the better. It is against such a background that the interpretations given by most Americans to the abstractions Freedom and Opportunity can be understood. Besides the right to do what one likes, when one likes, without the interference of authority, Freedom means, over and above everything else, Freedom to make more and better things, without external interference from government or sentimental do-gooders. Opportunity is opportunity for as large a proportion of the population as possible to engage in such activities. The political connotations of these abstractions are subservient to the creative ones, and are chiefly envisaged as the establishment of the political conditions which will give the creative capacities the greatest facilities.

These attitudes and beliefs are held unquestioningly by all except an insignificant group of intellectuals. An illuminating anecdote is told about the late President Roosevelt, on the occasion of a discussion of the ways of getting American literature and propaganda into the hands of the Russian people, in order to convert them from a totalitarian to a democratic way of life. After a prolonged discussion of some of the classical texts of American democracy, President Roosevelt is alleged to have said: "If I wanted to point out to the Russians the superiority of the American way of life, I should try to get just one book into their hands—the Sears-Roebuck catalogue."

Through the techniques of mass production, American men have produced more and better goods than the world has ever seen; but it is not as mass producers that Americans tend to think of themselves ideally. The ideal situation is envisaged as a man alone with his raw materials, using his industry, ingenuity, and know-how to make two blades of wheat grow where one grew before, to produce better mousetraps in ever-increasing quantity until they are available to everyone who has a mouse. This is the vision. This is the picture which accounts for the quasi-religious overtone given to the phrase "private enterprise." It is this which gave meaning and warmth to the slogans of the expansive twenties: "The business of America is business"; "What is good for business is good for America."

This ideal situation is now very rare, and it had ceased to be typical fifty years ago. But the fact that the reality is rare does not make the ideal less potent; most Americans believe that, whatever their own walk of life, America should be the land of the small and productive businessman (or would be if "government" or "big business" did not interfere), just as many Englishmen believe against all evidence that England is predominantly rural and that most people live in the country.

This picture of the present in terms of a past which has long since vanished, and the common aspiration to make the picture come true in the future, are essential clues to the understanding of much American political behavior, both foreign and domestic. Americans are in no doubt that this life of production, of making more and better things available to more and more people, is the good life; and with simple missionary zeal they wish to make it possible for the less fortunate, the benighted, to share it. Activities which foreigners interpret as subtle penetrations of American exploitative capital, and which may indeed have that effect, are usually purely benevolent in intention, attempts to free people from the laws and traditions which have prevented them from producing as they could and should, making it easy for American know-how to be communicated. Americans see themselves as a nation of businessmen, but not as a nation of big businessmen; business is creative and productive, big business restrictive and exploitative.

A friend of mine, who was at one time active in the anti-trust division of the Department of Justice and who was involved in a number of court injunctions against large companies, told me that, whatever the merits of the case, the lawyers of the companies arraigned spent most of their time trying to convince the juries that their company represented business, whereas the federal lawyers tried to prove that the company was big business. The details of the actual cases were usually far too intricate for an ordinary jury to understand; but their bias was uniformly in favor of business and hostile to big business, and the verdict was given according to the identification made.

It should further be noted that in the ideal picture the businessman, the producer, is alone with his raw materials, and that the only rules for dealing with the materials are pragmatic—the only test of fitness of treatment is in the result. Other people appear in this picture in the vaguest way, as the world beating a path to one's doorstep to reward one's ingenuity and industry. In the imagined golden age of equal independent producers no other relationship than that of willing buyer and willing seller was necessary or envisaged; but such a simplification, if it ever existed, has not existed for a long time; and so there is posed the great problem: What is the role of other men in the world of things?

As far as subordinate workers are concerned, the answer has usually been a compound of two contradictory components: a tendency to treat one's workers as things, and the emotional egalitarianism which makes any position of authority distasteful and which is typified by the worker and the employer calling each other by their Christian names and visiting each other's homes. Both components have existed as long as the United States; which aspect has been most stressed has depended on the period, on who the workers were, and generally on the size of the under-taking. The more the workers were patently alien, patently not-white-American, the greater the tendency to treat them as things. For nearly half its history chattel slavery was current in a great part of the United States, and the treatment generally accorded to the floods of immigrants up to 1924 approximated closely to the treatment of things, of raw material. Until the flow of immigrants dried to a trickle, so that most workers were Americans, until conservation became necessary, the rights legally accorded to the American worker were remarkably few; apart from the free education of his children there was practically no social-security legislation; and the attempts to form trade unions among semiskilled and unskilled workers were gen-erally suppressed with the greatest violence and the tacit approval of the rest of the community. The recent de-velopment of treating the worker as part of the machine has already been discussed. As a thing the worker is as amenable to efficient exploitation as any other raw mate-rial, and a number of scientific and pragmatic techniques have been developed for this. The "industrial efficiency experts" have developed ingenious techniques for prevent-ing the waste of the workers' muscular energy, in a manner analogous to that of industrial engineers preventing the wastage of heat; and the more recent developments of in-dustrial psychology have been successful in utilizing the workers' emotional life in the interests of greater productivity.

Concomitant with this, and in some areas and periods far more general, went the treatment of the subordinate worker as a complete equal and complete human being who—it was implied, if not expressed—through lack of opportunity was not yet an independent producer but who was shortly going to become one. In the earlier days of free land and small businesses this supposition was often justified. Under such circumstances the hired farm hand was often really treated as one of the family, the small manufacturer did know all his employees intimately, visited them when they were sick, helped them when they were in trouble, visited and was visited by them. This is the ideal and idyllic employer-employee relationship to which many American businessmen hark back nostalgically, and which is perpetuated in ghastly parodies by big corporations in office parties and company picnics. This was the picture that the elder Henry Ford tried so hard to realize in his enormous workshops, and which he eventually tried to impose through force. It is a picture which has still not lost all its glamor and appeal. Thus Henry Kaiser's treatment of his workers during the war—for example, the organization of a superior medical service—was felt to be in the good old American tradition. This tradition, it is perhaps necessary to emphasize, is not paternal; it is more nearly fraternal, the elder brother giving the kid brother a helping hand.

What signally failed to develop, at least up to 1929, was the viewing of the subordinate workers as a *class*, with definable positions, rights, and duties within the social structure. Objectively, of course, the workers could be so considered; but subjectively neither the greater number of employers nor the greater number of employees viewed them in that light. Until comparatively recently unions were few and their membership small, and such as existed were mostly craft unions; true, early attempts to form unions were often suppressed with great violence, but the early history of Western European unions is not one of unmitigated sweetness and light. Even today, when the majority of industrial workers are organized into trade unions and when the size of most industries makes the old fraternal picture an impossible dream, few workers appear to think of themselves as member of a sociopolitical class. America remains unique among highly industrialized countries in having no political party staffed by and representative of the trade unions. The American political system would make it very hard for such a "third party" to gain complete political power, at any rate immediately, but there is nothing inherent in the system which would prevent individual candidates from being elected. But even in the most militant section of the unions—the Political Action Committee of the Congress of Industrial Organizations—the demand for such a party has been slight and sporadic. Attempts to reproduce on American soil political parties based on the class assumptions of Europe have been ludicrous failures. The minute Socialist party receives almost more support from university professors than from workers; and the microscopic Communist party, apart from a very few "front" men, is almost entirely composed of inadequately assimilated immigrants and their children among the workers and white-collar classes and the "intelligentsia" of the largest cities. Significantly, the indigenous American radical movements, such as the I. W. W., the Populists, and the Farmer-Labor party, have chiefly been recruited from the rural or migrant population and have aimed at a restoration of the American dream of the past and the removal of the supposed excrescences thereon —the power of the bankers, symbolized by Wall Street, the expropriation of the small farmer and manufacturer, and the like. Some of the earlier movements tried to suppress such excrescences literally, by the use of dynamite; but, underlying such violence, was nearly always the picture of a return to a classless society, and not an attempt to improve the position of the working class within the existing society. The difference is profound; and in it lies the difference between the American "liberal" and the European "radical." The American "liberal" is trying to preserve the essence of the past, while the nonpolitical conservative wants more and more progress; the European conservative wants to preserve the past, and the "radical" wishes to hasten the transformation of the future. It is for this reason that the sympathies of nearly all Americans of good will can be aroused in the name of the "common man," and of relatively few in the name of the worker.

The typical patterns of the relationship between American employers and employees can be viewed as stemming from a shared abhorrence of the idea of one man being in overt authority over an equal. To avoid the appearance of authority in situations in which it was inherent, two solutions were found: stressing the fundamental equality of human beings outside the working situation, or, alternatively, denying to the inferior full status as a human being, treating him like a thing, in which case the only rule was efficient exploitation. Both these attitudes appear, often in sudden alternation, when Americans abroad are dealing with foreign peoples.

Fellow producers, competitors and rivals, could seldom be treated as things. They had to be treated as human beings and therefore as equals, in theory and in rights, however unequal they might be in resources and powers.

Between equals the normal relationship should be one of competition—friendly competition, ideally, but anyhow competition. And this competition is envisaged as one in which another man's gain is, inevitably, your loss; it is not envisaged, as it might have been, and as competition has been envisaged in other societies, as a situation in which everybody can win (the competition of the Caucus race) or even one in which the number of places at the top is indefinite, so that another person's success may be a spur rather than a challenge. If another person does better than you, you are humiliated, in so far as you accept the competition. The universal competition is tempered to the extent that, within limits, the individual may choose whom he will regard as his competitors and rivals. Provided he is realistic in his estimation of his own power and resources, the competition may well, as its advocates claim, be a source of stimulation to greater diligence and ingenuity; but if he is rash enough to challenge his superiors (or unfortunate enough to be involved in the plans of his superiors) he then deserves no mercy, and will get none. "Never give a sucker an even break" is the folk-saying which identifies and justifies such conduct. The sucker is the overcredulous person, the person who does not realize the difference between himself and those he challenges. His involvement in the situation is seen as voluntary, indeed as deliberately sought; and consequently he has nobody but himself to blame if he is ruined and destroyed. According to American ethics, it is morally wrong to attack a person weaker than oneself; but if the weaker attacks (or is provoked into attacking) it is not wrong to use all one's strength against him. The ideal of justice is reconciled with the recognition of inequality by the fiction that the weaker always has the choice of whether he will challenge the stronger or no.

It is probably this situation which helps account for one of the more striking paradoxes in the American world of business and of things. Although success is so vitally important for the individual that he will often literally work himself to death or to a nervous breakdown to attain, maintain and increase it, failure, especially sudden and dramatic failure—ruin—is not correspondingly disastrous. A complete setback need not, and generally does not, destroy all self-confidence. In the great depression of 1929–32 there were a number of spectacular suicides; less dramatic, but many times more numerous, were the equally ruined men who set about rebuilding their fortunes from nothing, using their dead selves as steppingstones to a new career. A slow decline is generally psychologically far more crippling than a complete disaster, for a slow decline suggests increasing incompetence, whereas disaster is a "bad break" in which the ego is not involved; it is viewed almost as though it were an "act of God" as described in insurance policies. A man is completely responsible for his own success; his failure is due to the acts of others.

The competition between near equals (or those supposed to be so) is regulated by the government, through the laws; indeed the chief, and for many the only essential, function of government is this regulation of competition. By and large, these regulations are not conceived of as moral imperatives, are not incorporated into the character; they are viewed rather as limitations and obstacles which should be treated with respect, but which a clever person may use to his advantage and, on occasion, get around. In so far as comparison with a sport is permissible, the more suitable would be all-in wrestling rather than boxing. An even more suitable comparison is poker, where each player is on his own, using all his wits to get the better of everybody else, and where success goes to him who combines most successfully skill, bluffing, luck, and resources. It is not surprising that poker is easily the favorite game of American businessmen (American workers seem to prefer games in which the element of luck is greater and that of skill less, such as throwing dice—craps) and that many metaphors of typical behavior are drawn from that game. Emotionally, too, American businessmen approach business with much of the zest with which they approach games; there is a sporting element in many business enterprises.

The metaphor of bluffing, a type of deceit which the

other players should expect and be prepared to meet, gives an important clue to the typical ethics of business. The fiats and prohibitions of the feminine conscience, dominant in all other spheres, are almost inoperative in business. Anyone who can "get away with" an infraction of the rules, especially the rules of government, without being caught or penalized is an object of admiration rather than of reprobation. Even the victims of such an infraction are not likely to resent such "slickness" deeply or long. The pragmatic test of success is always the final justification.

Because success is so overwhelmingly important, there is always a tendency for the rule-abiding majority to be pushed toward more and more questionable practices by the ingenious or unscrupulous minority. There is little sympathy, and less support, for a failure whose failure is due to a self-righteous refusal to follow a prevailing trend. The ethical may use every endeavor to get the rules strengthened and made more watertight; but people have little use for a man who squeals because another has been smarter than he. Business competition is regulated by temporary rules, rather than by permanent ethical principles.

Although the all-against-all of the poker game is the general condition of business competition, it may be modified by partnerships or associations. Two sorts of association are envisaged. One is the strictly *ad hoc* association of two or more competitors temporarily joining their resources to put a rival out of business, leaving their own competition in abeyance until the intruder has been removed from the field. Once this has occurred, the muted competition is resumed. The other type of partnership is that in which people join their different and complementary talents for their mutual advantage, as when one partner provides the patent and the other the capital. Partnerships are never thought of as similar to the temporary partnerships of such games as tennis or bridge. Partnerships should always be working partnerships.

The picture of competition between near-equal individuals as the general rule of American production and business is more a reference to a mythical past than a picture of the contemporary scene, where nearly every major industry is controlled by a few big corporations. But here again an image of an ideal world may be more potent in influencing contemporary conduct than the objectively viewed reality. This picture of free competition between near equals engendering ever more, cheaper, and better goods may be brandished by the public-relations officials of the big quasi-monopolies completely cynically, to prevent any further interference with their search for profits; but it is believed in good faith by the greater number of their audience, including most of the legislators. America has achieved unparalleled strength, wealth, and productivity in a very short time; this achievement of strength, wealth, and productivity was accompanied by almost unregulated competition: therefore, it is argued and believed, this almost unregulated competition is a prerequisite for further increase in strength, wealth, and productivity.

In the world of things, the world of American male supremacy, the only important human relationships are those between employer and employee, and those between competitors and rivals. There is a third relationship, that between the producer and the consuming public; this relationship is much less structured than the other two; but in so far as it is conceptualized, the public falls more into the category of things, of raw material, than into that of human beings. Continuing the mineral analogy, the purchasing power has to be extracted from the consuming public, as though it were silver being extracted from the baser ore. To achieve this efficiently the public is assayed and analyzed, using the increasingly refined techniques of market research. Once the possible yield has been determined, any device for flattering, cajoling, or bamboozling the public into yielding up its purchasing power is legitimate. The devices of advertising—perhaps most markedly in the case of TV—demonstrate a consistent and profound contempt for the public on the part of the advertisers and their employers. In the distorting mirror of advertising copy and TV commercials the public is shown to itself as naïve and puerile, driven by lust and greed and fear, without judgment or intellectual curiosity. For the producer the consumer is never an equal or near equal; fooling the public, "putting one over" on the consumer, is an act of which nobody need be ashamed; indeed it is a proper subject for boasting. Barnum made a boast of fooling the public: "A sucker is born every minute"; and Barnum is well on the way to becoming a folk hero.

VII

SUCCESS AND THE DOLLAR

FOR EVERY right-thinking American the object of life—indeed almost the justification for living—is to be a success, to "make good." To make good things, and more of them, is the best and most concrete way of making good, and is the reason for the very high prestige and respect accorded to the successful businessman, manufacturer, and engineer. But not all people can make things, and everyone should make good. When there are no things, how can one be sure that a person is a success?

This could be a very great problem in America because of the enormous diversity of pursuits inherent in a complex society, and because there is no accepted hierarchy of social values. Compared with the situation in Europe, the contrast between the prestige inherent in different professions and occupations is relatively slight. A few vocations have relatively low social prestige, especially when their esteem is compared with European countries—politics, the civil service, peacetime soldiering, teaching for men (it is essentially a somewhat feminine pursuit)—but this is because they are thought to be safe and easy, demanding too little initiative and tainted with the suspicion of authority, rather than from any absolute standards. Other things being equal, clean work is preferable to dirty work, a white-collar job to a shirt-sleeves job. But what makes other things equal? With the increasing lack of emotional involvement in most work, there is only one lowest common denominator by which jobs can be compared, by which success in one pursuit can be compared with success in quite a different one, and that is the social value accorded to each; and in a relatively unstructured commercial society this can only be measured in one way: in dollars.

From one aspect, dollars can be considered an adult equivalent of the marks and grades which signified the school child's relative position in regard to his fellows. An adult's income shows his rating in relation to his fellows, and a relatively good income is as much a matter for legitimate pride and boasting as getting A's in all subjects on one's report card. It is an outward and visible sign that one has striven successfully.

It should be emphasized that incomes are normally judged from a relative and not from an absolute standpoint. Grades are relative within the class: to get all A's in the first grade is as meritorious as to get all A's in the twelfth, but absolutely this does not mean that the work of the first grader is equal in value to the work of the twelfth grader; so, in the same way, the young doctor or typist is not measured against John D. Rockefeller, Jr., or Doris Duke (or whoever today has the highest income in the United States) but against other doctors starting in practice at the same time, other typists who have been in the office about the same time. Competition is still primarily among near equals.

The analogy with school life can be carried further. Just as in school, success in one grade qualifies one for entry into the tougher competition of the next grade, and so on indefinitely, so success in one area of adult life qualifies one for competition in the next "income bracket" or professional group. Success is always relative, never absolute. There are practically no positions in American life where it will be generally conceded that a person has achieved final success and need make no further effort. There is always a higher grade.

In childhood and youth good grades in school were rewarded by the love and praise of the parents, especially the mother; and consequently good grades quickly came to symbolize a promise of love. Dollars in adult life would seem to have something of the same function, signs that one is worthy of love and should receive it. And just as most Americans are insatiable for the personal signs of friendship and love, so do many appear insatiable for the dollars which are also the promissory notes of love. In the biographies of many of the conspicuously successful, a recurring theme is the stern upbringing or harsh childhood which forced them early to seek success.

In adult life there is one important modification in relative rating which is not easily paralleled from school: the past is an important factor in assessing present performance. Where incomes and positions are equal, greater respect is usually accorded to the man who has started with fewer advantages in parental wealth, education, and opportunity; outside the South and, to a much lesser extent,

New England, Mr. Bounderby is more worthy of respect than Mr. Gradgrind.

This "rating" aspect of money is for Americans, at least for the two thirds who are not "ill-fed, ill-clothed, ill-housed," at least as important as any of the uses to which it can be put. Of course the purchasing power of the dollar is important for securing the basic necessities of life (and these are variously defined); but once these have been secured, its social value is at least as great as its purchasing power.

It is this doubly symbolic value of the dollar which makes the American attitude toward money so paradoxical to the European. To phrase it briefly, Americans talk far more about money than Europeans and generally value it far less. Incomes and prices are of great social importance for rating people and goods in relation to one another; until you know the income bracket of a stranger, and he knows yours, your mutual relationship is unsatisfactory and incomplete; and the easiest method of evaluating a strange article and putting it into relationship with other articles is to know what it cost. As a result, money and prices figure greatly and consistently in American writing and conversation; the income bracket of an individual or the cost of an article is a necessary and useful piece of social information; to inform a stranger on such points, when he is likely to be ignorant, is an act of neighborliness.

It is a great mistake, however, to deduce from the fact that Americans pay so much verbal attention to money the supposition that they give corresponding importance to the possession of money, as such. The contrary is more nearly true; compared with most Europeans, Americans rate the possession, and above all the retention, of money very low. Income—the money that comes in to you—fixes your relative position in regard to your fellows; but once it has done that, it has fulfilled its chief purpose, and there is no deep emotional reason for retaining it. Saving, except for the purpose of putting money back in one's business and thereby increasing one's future income, is not laudable; a prudent man will have some cushion against unexpected illness or misfortune; but saving, as an aim in itself, is not regarded as praiseworthy today, a marked change from earlier attitudes. The contrast with the attitude of such peoples as the Scots or the French, for whom saving has or had an almost automatic virtue, is very marked.

The financial duties expected of an American whose income exceeds his necessary expenditures are defined and limited. He should "carry" enough life insurance to make certain that, should he die suddenly, his wife and children should not be in want; he should, either by insurance or by saving, provide for his children the best possible education, preferably better than he had enjoyed himself; he should not let his parents, or his spouse's, suffer actual want; and he may buy an annuity against his retirement. That is all. There is no demand or expectation that an American, whatever his fortune, should leave substantial sums to his children; provided he has brought them to adulthood with every advantage he can give them, he has done the whole of his duty toward them. Indeed, inherited money can in some respects be regarded as a handicap; with such a head start, a man has to make correspondingly much more before he can be considered to have made good, to be a success. With the partial exception of New York and its satellite resorts, there is no place or position anywhere in American life for the young man of inherited means who is not gainfully employed. Before the war a small number used to emigrate to Europe, where there was still a cosmopolitan leisure class; but these were exceptions, and the general practice was and is for millionaires' and multi-millionaires' sons to go into business (preferably one with which the father has no connection, to avoid the suspicion of favoritism, of having things easy) and make their own money, prove their own worth in the competition of life.

It can be said that, as a general rule, the acquisition of money is very important to Americans, but its retention relatively unimportant. One's worth is confirmed by every extra dollar one brings in, and therefore, in the way of business, the harder the bargain one strikes the more one is worthy of respect and so of love; but once the money has been brought in, it loses much of its emotional importance; it can be spent, or given away or, figuratively, thrown into the gutter without deep involvement or regret; it only becomes important again if it is used in another business transaction, for then it again becomes a test of one's shrewdness, one's acumen, one's success.

This attitude is almost certainly an important component in American gambling. American gambling differs from European not in its diffusion—there is probably a greater proportion of small gamblers in most European countries—but in its intensity. Probably because of the relative unimportance of retaining money, Americans at nearly all income levels will risk a far greater proportion of the money they hold in wagers and gambling games than most of their European equivalents. The term of opprobrium for a timid gambler—"piker"—has no common equivalent in any Western European language. In gambling "for fun" most Americans will risk proportionately far more than most Europeans. To determine that one's "luck is in" is as good a use for money as another.

Gambling is also a respected and important component in many business ventures. Conspicuous improvement in a man's financial position is generally attributed to a lucky combination of industry, skill, and gambling, though the successful gambler prefers to refer to his gambling as "vision." Like the gambler "for fun" the American businessman is generally prepared to take proportionately far greater risks than his European equivalent.

Gambling apart, few people in the world are less involved in the destination of their money than the Americans, provided there is no suggestion of a business transaction, in which one's ego is necessarily implicated; and no people in the world give their money away with greater ease.

American generosity and hospitality are rightly famous. In no other country does the majority of the citizens give so easily and freely, almost without counting the cost. In the summer of 1940, when there were plans for sending to

America large numbers of English children from the threatened invasion, a quite astonishing number of American families from every region and every income level were ready to accept, as it seemed then for the rest of their lives, responsibility for threatened children whom they had never seen and of whom they knew nothing except that they were threatened. Similarly, when Tokyo was partially destroyed by the 1923 earthquake, it was in great part rebuilt by money given by millions of Americans, the vast majority of whom had never seen a Japanese. These instances are conspicuous, but they could be reduplicated very many times. For any cause that can be considered worthy, Americans will give their money with the greatest generosity, and not merely out of their superfluity; in many cases such gifts are made at the expense of considerable personal sacrifice.[1]

This great and ungrudging generosity is limited by one fear: the suspicion that one may be being exploited, "made a sucker." Maybe the claimant on one's charity is feckless rather than in want, wishing to live lazily on the money one has worked so hard to get, refusing to make the efforts and undergo the privations one has had to make and undergo oneself.

This suspicion is very general, especially among American men (it would seem to be much less strongly de-

---

[1] Incidentally, Americans give their money with very much greater ease than they give their food. Whereas money, once it has been acquired, loses much of its importance, the quasi-magical values of good American food remain constant; money, in most cases, can be replaced with relative ease; but if there were a shortage of food one would not only be depriving oneself, one would be threatening the future of one's children.

veloped among women). The reason for the general prevalence of this fear is obscure to me; I would suggest tentatively that it is linked with the already discussed obsessive American fear of lapsing into passivity; of being exploited physically in the one case, financially in the other. Among the American men of my acquaintance, those who were most prone to such suspicions in the financial sphere showed clear indications of having such unconscious fears also; and the metaphors so frequently used in such contexts (America being sexually exploited) bear out the supposition.

When this suspicion is not aroused, American money is given freely and without afterthought, and American hospitality is without self-consciousness and with a certain pride. In those houses—the vast majority—where people normally eat in the kitchen (or a dining nook just off the kitchen) the stranger is warmly welcomed, without ostentation and without shame. In the dining-room class pretension and the maneuvering for social advantage are more likely to be evident; after a certain financial status has been obtained and demonstrated, other methods of scoring relative success may be called into play: ancestry, creed, length of residence of oneself or one's ancestors in the town, in the state, in the country can all be used as scoring points in the fight for success once the financial status is, or has been, established.

The chief emotional value of one's money income is as a sign of one's relative success; but though in theory a certified pay check would be adequate, in practice one can only demonstrate the fact that one has made good by con-

spicuous expenditure. Consequently every possession becomes doubly important, not only for its own use or
beauty, but as a palpable symbol of its owner's or pur-
chaser's relative position in the competition of life. A new
car is not desirable and enviable merely because it is better
(few Americans would question that "new" and "better"
were synonyms) but also because it is an outward and
visible sign of an inward and spiritual grace; the man who
can afford or acquire a new car demonstrates to the world
that he is making good—and "good" has a moral as well as
a material significance.

The pattern of competitive conspicuous expenditure is
summed up in one current, almost proverbial, phrase:
"Keeping up with the Joneses." One significant implica-
tion of this phrase is that competition could not easily be
less clearly defined. The Joneses are undefined regionally,
socially, locally, ethnically (Anglo-Saxon surnames were
often provided by the immigration officers to new arrivals
with unpronounceable names; it would be rash to suppose
that an American Jones had Welsh ancestors); they are
the people one has to keep up with, and only inspection
can demonstrate in a given instance who they are.

As a general rule it can be said that in the smaller towns
(up to, say, fifty thousand inhabitants) and in the suburbs
the Joneses are one's neighbors, in the larger towns, people
engaged in similar pursuits and holding similar positions.
Each family has its own "Joneses" and is itself a "Jones"
for others. Just as in the childhood world of the play group,
the parents of one's children's playmates set a standard
with which it was difficult not to conform, so, in the adult

world of conspicuous expenditure, the Joneses influence, not only how much one will spend, but what one will spend it on.

This is true at almost every level of income and social aspiration. At the lowest level of subsistence the possibility of choice is obviously extremely limited; and among the very rich, or those whose ancestors were very rich, the pattern takes an idiosyncratic form. Between these two extremes, the proper expenditure at any level of income in any given area is defined with remarkable exactness and precision.

In any city the price and the social value (which may not completely correspond) of any house on any street is well known to the greater number of the inhabitants, and this information will be freely passed on to any stranger. As a consequence the neighborhood and the house in which a person lives are an immediate and patent sign of his income, and income, far more than taste, will in most cases and under normal circumstances indicate where a person's residence shall be. Except among the very rich or the descendants of rich ancestors (and with the partial exception of anomalous intellectuals and artists) the place where one lives is valued as a symbol of one's current economic and social position, and not (at least in the first instance) for any amenities inherent in it or associations attached to it. The majority of Americans, at least until they near the retirement age, regard themselves as transient inhabitants of their house or apartment, ready to move to the bigger and better dwelling which will be appropriate to the greater success hoped for in the future.

The vast majority of urban Americans are transient; before the current housing difficulties, it was an exceptional person who had lived in the same place for five years. This mobility accounts for the peculiar significance given by Americans to the word "home"; "home" is a place where one would like to live, at least as much as it is the place where one is living at present; the term is applied consistently to the more desirable houses in a neighborhood. A neighborhood may be described as consisting of "lovely homes" by a person who has never been inside one of the houses so commended.

To a great extent, the residence dictates a great number of other conspicuous expenditures. Few Americans, without elaborate explanations and excuses, would dare have only one car in a house which has a two-car garage. In the normal American house (as opposed to the apartment) nearly everything is open to the inspection of the world; no hedges, walls, or gates separate the building from the road; and though the shades are generally halfway down during the day, even though there be no glare, they are also halfway up at night, and some of the furnishings of most lighted rooms can be detailed from the street. Incidentally, this proper position of the shades has an almost fetishist importance; cases have been recorded of people with an excessive desire for light being asked to surrender their lease because the furled shades in one house lowered the appearance of the whole neighborhood. Even in apartments the conformity is generally great; there is an often repeated story of the tenant in 13-B visiting the tenant in 2-B and telling her her furniture was in the wrong place.

Not only the cost but also the style of furniture and domestic appliances are controlled by the Joneses. American women—for decoration is by general consensus an exclusively feminine interest—take good taste very seriously; they attend lectures on the subject and read magazine articles about it (and many of the women's magazines have circulations running into the millions); in the more prosperous groups, a woman's taste is almost a complement to her husband's earning capacity as an index of comparative social success. These standards, needless to say, are abetted and enhanced by the manufacturers and advertisers. The result is twofold. The average standard of taste in the furnishings of nearly all American homes at almost any income level is remarkably high, and the similarities between the furnishings of homes of the same income level is equally remarkable. It is rare in American homes to come across that crowded absence of taste which distinguishes so many European interiors; and it is almost equally rare to come across a house with decorations distinctive enough to be remembered apart from its peers for more than a few days. The decorations of a house are meant to "express the woman's personality"; but these personal expressions are normally limited to relatively slight variations in the color scheme and the choice of the smaller ornaments; any major variation is either an affront to the Joneses, by rejecting the accepted standards, or else a challenge to rivals; in which case the innovator becomes the "Jones" whom the rivals will attempt to equal and surpass as soon as their means allow.

Among those who are building their position, the most modern is the most desirable, though a woman may "express her personality" by collecting small antique objects; but at the top of the social or economic hierarchy these values are reversed, and furniture and domestic appliances become esteemed to the extent that they are not modern, not labor saving. Since trained domestic servants are (outside the Negroes of the South) rare and highly paid, the demonstration that one has no need to rely on labor-saving devices is one of the most impressive methods of advertising one's income, one's success. Moreover, when incomes are relatively large and relatively equal, additional scoring points can be made on the grounds of ancestry; and articles of furniture which can be ascribed to grandparents or great-aunts advance a permanent claim for respect from those less well-ancestored or with fewer generations of American-born forebears. It is worth noting in this connection that an interest in genealogy, like an interest in decoration or in flowers, is considered essentially feminine, and unworthy of a proper man, who should be judged on his achievements alone.

As with decoration, so with clothes and personal adornment. A man is known by his wife's fur coat. American methods of mass production have been as successfully applied to clothes as to more durable articles; and women, save for those at the very top and very bottom of the social scale, who do not dress in the current fashion can be regarded as lowering the tone of the neighborhood. The store patronized, the material used, and innumerable more subtle touches will indicate clearly enough to other women the level of expenditure; but the current fashion is attainable at a great range of income levels and can be safely ignored only by the poorest and the richest.

The face and figure should approximate as closely as possible to that of the Joneses. Individual variations there cannot help but be, but they should be minimized as much as possible. Diet, exercises, massage, girdles and other "foundation garments," false breasts, can modify irregularities of the figure; permanent waves (or, in the case of Negroes, straightening), variations in the hair; the excellent American dentists make discolored or uneven teeth a sign of poverty or of unsocial behavior; make-up, hand creams, nail polish take care of the uniformity of the skin, deodorants and perfumes of any individual exhalation. Here again, the necessary commodities are within the reach of nearly every income. All the necessary ingredients and appliances can be bought at the five-and-ten (and, according to *Consumer's Union*, often the best); inspection of the advertisement pages of the *New Yorker* or such luxury magazines as *Vogue* or *Harper's Bazaar* shows how much can be paid for similar articles and appliances. One brand of scent advances as the only reason why anybody should buy it the fact that it is "the costliest perfume in the world."

Until the last fifteen years, such detailed physical conformity was more demanded from women than from men; but today there is increasing stress on male beauty treatments. Padded shoulders and shoes with hidden elevators can alter some of the unnecessary variations of nature, and masculine cosmetics (delicately referred to as "toiletries") are a great and growing industry.[2]

Even children can be molded nearer to the proper pattern. It is not uncommon for girls to get their first permanent wave at the age of four, and even younger tots can occasionally be seen with tinted finger nails. This latter adornment may be more in the nature of playing at being grown up than serious make-up, but the other beautifications are in earnest.

Because of the relative uniform structure of American society, and because success is only defined in relative, and not absolute, terms, everything that a man has, or is responsible for, becomes important as an index of his status and position. And because there are few absolute standards of value, of desirability, or of beauty, the way most likely to win the envy and approval of one's neighbors and rivals—the goal and object of life—is to approximate as closely as possible to the standards they have adopted, but to attempt to be a little bit bigger, a little bit better.

[2] *Time*, American Overseas edition, March 10, 1947, speaks of the "$50,000,000-a-year men's toiletries market" in discussing the launching of a new "carnation-scented, flesh-colored paste which will camouflage 5 o'clock shadow and banish that unshaven look." In its first week the company sold about 57,000 jars of its camouflage at a dollar apiece.

VIII

MORE EQUAL THAN OTHERS

AMERICANS differ from the rest of the world in their belief that nationality is an act of will, rather than the result of chance or destiny. The message of General Patton, already quoted, made the point with admirable succinctness when he contrasted his troops' ancestors "who so loved freedom that they gave up home and country to cross the ocean in search of liberty" with the ancestors of the enemy who "lacked the courage to make such a sacrifice and continued as slaves." In the view of General Patton, and probably of the greatest part of his audience and compatriots, the fact that the Germans and the Italians were Germans and Italians rather than Americans was a sign of their (and their ancestors') weakness of will and their contumacy; by not *choosing* to be American they had willfully rejected the best condition known to men and all its attendant advantages; they had shown individually their contempt for and their rejection of Freedom, Opportunity, Democracy, and all the other civic virtues embodied in the American Constitution and exemplified in the American Way of Life; from weakness of spirit they had chosen to be inferior, and should therefore be so regarded.

This view is still very generally held. Although during

the last quarter of a century various laws have reduced the flood of immigration to a trickle, few Americans who are not personally involved realize how stringent the quotas are; and, particularly in the big cities, the number of people talking with a foreign accent and reading foreign-language newspapers is still sufficiently large to keep vivid this picture of nationality by choice. The acquisition of American nationality by famous or notorious authors, scientists, film stars, and the like is a constantly recurring item of news.[1] The belief is further kept vivid by annual nation-wide ceremonies in the spring, marking I Am an American Day, in which speeches (generally broadcast) are made on the significance of Americanism and the current crop of new citizens are welcomed. The affirmation I Am an American is not however meant to be confined to those who have a right to make it for the first time; in theory it should be fervently and thankfully repeated by everyone who has the right to do so. In the case of the vast majority of schoolchildren this affirmation is made personally; and the celebrations of the Day come as a culmination of the important courses in civics which have taught them the implications of this proud boast, and of the daily rituals, such as the Salute to the Flag, which should engrave the precepts in their minds and in their hearts.

This affirmation and celebration differ in quality from those made by some other peoples through their emphasis

---

[1] American citizenship is still today more easily acquired than that of any other major country; five years' residence after having made a Declaration of Intention and a relatively simple examination in American history and the Constitution are all that is demanded from the literate.

on the individual will and act of choice. The nearest parallel was probably the Japanese celebration of the festival of Jimmu Tenno; but though the Japanese were as articulate as the Americans about the advantages and merits of being a member of their own society, they ascribed this membership to the Will of the Gods. For the Japanese, until their defeat, it was other people's misfortune to belong to inferior societies, but not their fault. For Americans, this misfortune is their own fault.

The historical reasons underlying the development of such an attitude are easily understandable. America is unique in that its citizenry (with the notable exception of the Negroes) is composed of people who either directly, or through their ancestors, did make this personal act of choice and, for the greatest part, in making it left behind not only bad material and social conditions but all that had made life dear and meaningful to them. America has never welcomed particularly warmly poor foreigners who speak bad or no English, and who have no title, reputation, or highly prized skill; and there can have been few immigrants who did not have moments of doubt as to the wisdom of their choice, who were not homesick for their families and for the better-known ways they had left behind. In an appreciable number of cases these immigrants did return to their homes; but those who did not must still the doubts and homesickness. Any public complaint or criticism was greeted with the snarl: "If you don't like it here, why don't you go back where you came from?" And the snarl was the more venomous when the utterer, as very often happened, himself spoke with a foreign accent; for the voiced complaints stirred his own hidden doubts and discomfort, and tended to make meaningless the immigrant's life, all his efforts and sacrifices. To compensate and crush any uncertainty the positive affirmation must be made as loudly, as stridently as possible; in no particular could it be admitted that what had been abandoned was equal or superior to what had been embraced; everything in American life—not merely its clear superiorities but everything—must be loudly proclaimed to be better than that which had been abandoned.

As comparison with American newspapers of fifty or a hundred years ago will easily demonstrate, the greater part of this stridency has been muted with the diminution of the number of first-generation Americans in the population. But it is still there and, significantly enough, most blatant in those areas with the biggest concentration of foreign born; the largely alien populations of New York and Chicago do much to explain the isolationist chauvinism and the huge circulations of the Chicago *Tribune* and the New York *Daily News.*

Although the stridency has been so much muted, the explicit statement of the superiority of all aspects of American life over all aspects of European life was generally easily accepted by the native-born Americans who for the greatest part had no opportunity (nor desire) to make comparisons with reality. Moreover all who lived in, or even visited, cities could see that the lives of those most freshly from Europe were inferior, in every tangible aspect, to those of most of their American compatriots and hosts.

There has been a consistent and understandable tendency throughout the whole history of immigration for newcomers to settle as closely as possible to former compatriots. From them alone could they expect help and guidance in a strange land and aid in earning a living. There, too, they could eat the accustomed food, hear the accustomed songs, speak their mother tongue, obtain some emotional warmth in a strange and alien world. As individual efforts at self-improvement were crowned with success they tended to move away from these foreign quarters, to mingle as unobtrusively as possible with the majority; and most of their children, as they were turned into Americans, rejected with vehemence everything which recalled the incomplete Americanism of their parents.

Naturally enough, the poor immigrants were housed in the least desirable slums, their poverty often forcing them to live under conditions of great and unsanitary overcrowding. Their unimportance as taxpayers and voters generally meant that they had the worst and least municipal services. The Little Italies, the Little Polands, the Chinatowns, the Greek, Jewish, Lithuanian, Serbian, Ukrainian and Irish quarters of most American towns are urban abominations which, apart from occasional "picturesqueness," cannot fail to fill the viewer who lives in an even slightly more favored locality with abhorrence and disgust. It was from these horrid slums that the generations of native-born Americans formed their picture of Europe; and in none was the abhorrence and disgust greater than in those who had just escaped from such environments. It is perhaps worth noting that the English and Scotch immigrants, with no language difficulty to make them dependent on the aid of their compatriots and, as Protestants, with no need for a religious confessor or spiritual guide with whom they must communicate in their own language, usually dispersed immediately and almost invisibly in the American community, and that the Germans and Scandinavians brought with them habits of cleanliness, civic tidiness, and a high standard of material comfort which made a marked distinction between their quarters and those of the immigrants from Southern and Eastern Europe and Asia.

The presence of these groups of immigrants—in many cases the shameful kin of hundred per cent Americans—was a major determinant in the definition of what was "Americanism." These people were patently not Americans, but they, or at least their children, were going to become Americans; and consequently Americanism was defined, to a very great extent, in terms of the outward and visible contrasts between these alien slum dwellers and what their children might achieve, the signs of a successful American.

The slums, the actual setting, were of great emotional importance. They were offensive to the senses and dangerous to the health, in actual fact as well as in the teaching and precepts of the schoolmistress. And so proper plumbing, toilets that worked, spotless bathrooms, light and clean kitchens, all types of labor-saving devices became not only desirable in themselves but signs of completer Americanism, of acceptance of the standards of the country which everybody, either in person or through their ancestors, had adopted. The symbolic and patriotic value of these adjuncts to sanitary and comfortable living has become so great that Americans in foreign countries tend to esteem these alien societies in direct proportion to the number and availability of these amenities, the country with the greater number being the more admirable, as more nearly approaching the American ideal. This standard was the cause of a great deal of unhappy confusion among those Americans who were sent to Europe in the last war, for at least one enemy, Germany, was far more "American" than any of the Allies; and the plumbing of some of the Allies compared unfavorably with the worst slums of which they had any personal experience.

Although these appliances are diffused far more widely in the United States than in any European country, there are still considerable areas outside the immigrants' quarters (and the even more horrible Negro slums) without constant hot water, perfect plumbing, or the other domestic appliances; but since Americanism is what one may become, even more than what one is, the young American soldier who exclaims, when confronted with an English suburb or French village, "No American would live in houses like these!" is perfectly sincere, even though his own youth may have been spent in a cold-water walk-up flat, or in a wooden cabin with no water except from a well, and plumbing reduced to an outhouse—a perennial topic for American humor. Whatever his actual conditions, his aspirations demand a truly American setting.

Appearance and clothes are other most important criteria of Americanism. That language should be a criterion is self-evident; and, having regard to the quasi-magical importance attached to food, it is not surprising that diet should also have evidential value. The overspiced and over-greasy foods of the various "old countries" are tolerable for a change; but as daily fare they are injurious to health, and show a failure to accept the modern and scientific principles of American living. The most important criterion of all, however, is undoubtedly appearance. The completeness of Americanization is directly correlated with the similarity in appearance between the person who is being judged and his or her American peers in age and income. To the extent that a person is identifiable as different in a crowd, to that extent is he or she incompletely American; and those whose skin color or physical conformation makes it impossible for them to merge into the crowd are thereby debarred from ever being considered fully American. The conforming surface is not only important as a means of keeping up with the Joneses; it is an essential component of true Americanism. It is only a slight exaggeration to say that a young woman who didn't paint her finger nails today would not be able to proclaim "I Am an American" with as much conviction and fervor as her properly made-up sisters.

Ideology is a minor component of Americanism, for what one thinks is far less important (and far less easy to judge) than what one does and how one appears. The rejection of authority is so basic that it can hardly be counted as ideological, though it has its ideological components; otherwise all that is needful is assent to the statement that the American Constitution and mode of government are (like the plumbing or the automobiles) the best in the world. Intolerance, racial discrimination, terrorism, are perfectly compatible with Americanism; such behavior is deeply deplored, and often most vigorously fought against by many, perhaps most, Americans, whose ideals of justice and equality are outraged when such qualities are manifested; but the members of the Ku Klux Klan, of the Knights of the White Camellia, of the numerous anti-Negro, anti-Jewish, and anti-Catholic organizations which flourish in the United States do not feel themselves to be other than American, and, except in a limited ethical sense, are not felt to be so by other Americans. Indeed it is not without significance that almost without exception the justification and charter of these organizations are the protection of Americanism from corruption by subversive and alien persons and influences.

The attainment of complete Americanism is judged principally by the eye, only secondarily by the ear. The position of minorities in America can only be understood if it is remembered that the criteria for Americanism are, in descending order of importance, appearance, clothes, food, housing amenities, ideology, and language, and that only the fully American can be considered fully human; for, be it remembered, Americanism is an act of will, and failure to achieve complete Americanism is an individual fault much more than it is a misfortune.

The crucial test of the concept of Americanism is the case of the American Negro. By any test of length of residence of the family in the country, of language, of ideology, American Negroes have better claims for complete Americanism than most of their white compatriots; but only the most unrealistic egalitarian would claim that this is conceded to them as a group, though the legal and civil disabilities under which they suffer are less in some parts of the country than in others. Outside the South a few Negroes have attained positions of considerable prestige and respect, but the vast majority have never been granted completely human status. A certain number of cross-breeds, whose Negro status is purely sociological, manage every year to "pass" into the white community, where they are granted full human rights because they cannot be distinguished by appearance from other Americans; but the remainder, who can be so distinguished, are systematically excluded from the main stream of American life, no matter how great a proportion of their ancestry was white (a Negro without an admixture of some white blood is a relative rarity in America), how complete their education, or how fervent their adherence to democratic principles. Despite the well-meaning and sincere social mixing of a few "liberals," intellectuals, and jazz enthusiasts, the general judgment is quite simply that Negroes look different and therefore are different.

The character of the Negroes is systematically distorted by the fact that they live in a world in which authority is continuously, though apparently capriciously, hostile; to teach their children to live safely in such a world, good Negro parents have to be continuously but apparently capriciously violent; physical punishment is used to a very great extent in the upbringing of Negro Americans, very little in the upbringing of whites. It would be possible, at least in theory, to develop undistorted personalities, even under such a regime, if the regime were accompanied by a consistent and adequate ideology; but the Negroes, even in the deepest South, are only taught the egalitarian ideology of the white American, so that their daily life seems riddled with injustice, and they permanently feel resentment they are not permitted to express. This suppressed resentment, even when it is not fully conscious, has obvious destructive social potentialities, which provide a rational justification for the fear which is felt by most white Americans, though it normally only attains an obsessive quality in the South, and which assures the perpetuation of the treatment which will produce the resentment. A few experiences of mixed white and Negro battalions and merchant ships during the war suggest that, at least among the young, the resentment becomes manageable almost as soon as authority ceases to be hostile; but as far as I know there have been no such experiments with groups of both sexes, and the sexual aspect—the exploitation of Negro women by white men, and the fear of complementary action—is crucial in the relationship of white and Negro. Although recent judgments of the Supreme Court have somewhat lessened the legal disabilities of the Negro in the South, the time is not foreseeable when most white Americans will not feel frightened and humiliated at having Negroes as immediate neighbors, even in a restaurant, and will not therefore have laws, or customs with the strength of law, to keep them away. Over a long enough period the surface characteristics which label the Negro as un-American will probably be bred out, if the society maintains its present form; but until that distant event occurs, the white criteria for full Americanism and full humanity will continue to distort the personalities of a tenth of the citizens of the United States. By all such scientific tests as are available, the potentialities of the Negroes do not differ from those of their white fellow citizens; but, with very few exceptions, the only major contribution they have been allowed to make to American culture is their music. The plaintive and derisive songs of an oppressed group have, chiefly in adaptations, become the background of the whole society's pleasures and distractions.[2]

The role of the other colored groups (with the partial exception of the Mexicans in the West and Southwest) is intermediate between that of the wholly excluded Negro and that of the wholly included White. In so far as they are visibly different they are excluded from full participation in the society (the number of jobs open to an American of Japanese or Chinese ancestry is limited) but their appearance is so much less distinctive than that of the Negro, and their numbers so relatively small, that the only major restriction applied to them is in leasing or buying houses and land. The neighborhood is such an important index of relative social position that the admission of in-

[2] Nearly every fact of sociological importance about the American Negro is contained in Gunnar Myrdal's *American Dilemma* (Harper, New York, 1944). The clearest psychological insight into the Negro character is given by Richard Wright's moving autobiography *Black Boy* (Harper, New York, 1945). Much information can also be gained from John Dollard's *Caste and Class in a Southern Town* (Yale University Press, 1937) and from Allison Davis' and John Dollard's *Children of Bondage* (American Council on Education, 1940). The last two books are occupied exclusively with the Deep South.

complete Americans into houses or apartments similar to those inhabited by complete Americans would sensibly lower the standing of the latter. In some areas nonwhites are also provided with separate schools and excluded from the rest.

The case of the Mexicans in Texas, and to a certain extent the adjoining states, is peculiar in several respects. Texans do not share with any deep emotion the anti-authoritarian egalitarianism of their fellow Americans, and feel no more guilt in keeping an alien and conquered group in a subservient position than do Europeans in African and Asian colonies. Moreover, the Mexicans have a civilization, a religion, and a language of their own, and not merely, as do the Negroes, more or less distorted versions of those of the whites. The Mexicans of Texas suffer from many of the disabilities of the Negroes in the South, they are mostly ill-housed, ill-clothed, ill-fed, and ill-paid; but they are an oppressed people with a method of life and a system of values which give meaning and support, not oppressed individuals whose experience is at complete variance with their values.

Since Americans refuse to recognize that they own an empire, the inhabitants of what are euphemistically called "Territories" or "Possessions" are in a peculiar position when they live in the United States. They are not allowed to become citizens, since, in an unreal legal way they are sort of citizens already; the obviously distinguishable Filipinos are chiefly confined to the most menial positions. They are fewer and more scattered than the Mexicans, and their dilemma more nearly approaches that of the

Negroes, for they too, most of them, have been taught the egalitarian theory which in their cases is seldom carried out in practice.

In many ways the cruellest position is that of the American children of Chinese and especially of Japanese parents. During the latter half of the nineteenth and the earlier years of the twentieth century—until they were legally excluded—Japanese and Chinese immigrated—particularly on the west coast—with exactly the same intentions and hopes as the immigrants from Europe. With even greater thoroughness than most of the Europeans—in part due to the greater obvious difference between their countries of birth and their country of allegiance—they set about turning their children into Americans with, in the vast majority of cases, complete success. By every criterion of Americanism, except that of physical appearance, the second-generation Japanese and Chinese were usually indistinguishable from their compatriots—their clothes, food, housing amenities (as far as this was possible), ideology, and language were so completely American that they did not even possess or envisage any alternative. But their appearance damned them; in almost any competition they were handicapped; their possibilities of employment in any mixed profession were always limited; entirely because they did not look American, they were denied full American, and therefore full human, status. This was dramatically illustrated in the months following Pearl Harbor, when full citizens of Japanese ancestry were deprived of all civic rights and herded into concentration camps (relocation camps), with a minimum of protest even from the professional defenders of civil liberties. No parallel action was taken against the children of German or Italian parents; since they were undistinguishable, they were treated as fully American and fully human.

The social position of the Jews is more complicated. The majority of American Jews come from Eastern Europe—Poland, Lithuania, Galicia, and Russia—and many of these possess a recognizable physical type. This physical type does not, however, deviate from the standard American appearance more than does that common among children of southern Italian or Greek parentage, and, by itself, would almost certainly not have evoked any more discrimination against or denial of full Americanism to the descendants of one group than to those of the others. But the Jews also brought with them deviant social habits which, because they were theocratically sanctioned, were maintained with far more emphasis in the new society than the "old-world" habits of other immigrant groups. Of these probably the most important, in its relation to American values, were the peculiar rules concerning the preparation and combination of foods, which in many instances went directly counter to American theory and practice. The insistence on this type of diet was a studied rejection of Americanism in one of its emotionally more important aspects. An inspection of the advertisements for hotels and holiday camps in the Sunday editions of the New York *Times* and other New York papers shows that this discrimination against American habits is still prevalent, for a sizable number still offer "dietary laws."

In a number of other instances the Jews rejected common American practice—in their maintenance of a calendrical pattern of fasts and feasts which were not shared by the rest of the community, in the reversal of Saturdays and Sundays, in the great importance given to claims of kinship in business and commercial life. The prohibition against mixed marriages could be paralleled in Catholic practice, but American Catholics come from a far greater variety of European backgrounds than American Jews and the limitation on the preferred marriage-by-choice among Jews was apparently greater. The rigid dietary laws prevented the pious immigrants from accepting the hospitality of their gentile neighbors and colleagues; and in many cases they forbade their children to eat with their schoolmates and insisted on their maintaining their differences. In short, during the period of greatest immigration and Americanization, the Jews were marked out from their fellow immigrants by their rejection of important aspects of American behavior, rather than, as far as can be gathered from existing records, by any concerted intention to exclude them on the part of gentile Americans.

It is against this background of the eclectic acceptance of American standards by the Jewish immigrants that the present position of Jews in America must be understood. The Jews had advanced claims in excess of any other immigrant group, basing them on theological sanctions which were not accepted by the rest of the community; they claimed all the advantages of full American citizenship without being willing to abandon those "old-world" habits and customs whose abandonment was, in the case of all other immigrants, a *sine qua non* of being granted full American status.

This claim for special privilege was not conceded willingly or ever in full. Complete legal equality was granted, but social equality was denied; since the Jews refused to abandon the un-American habits which all other groups, however painfully, had given up, they were treated as incomplete Americans; their exclusion was followed by a counterexclusion; and, in the common pattern of American exclusion, this was above all manifested in the renting and selling of houses, in the preservation of the neighborhood from "foreign-ness." The holiday camps and hotels with the "dietary laws" were counterbalanced by "restricted" hotels, holiday camps, and neighborhoods.

Despite this incomplete participation, many Jews were markedly successful in the varied competitions which make up American life, whether in school, in established professions, in government, in business, or in the new industries which have developed in the last fifty years. Since success is so generally equated with love, it seemed as though the Jews were more loved by the authorities— whether schoolmistress, government, or some abstract Fortune—than their gentile fellow citizens; and the latter tended to resent this apparent unfairness.

Many of the children and nearly all the grandchildren of the original immigrants were willing to abandon in a considerable degree these claims for special status, and in greatest part gave up completely the un-American habits which were the manifestation of such claims. But the special status which had originally been demanded was now imposed; the grandparents had emphasized their differentness by claiming special rights and immunities; the grandchildren abandoned these claims but differentness was thrust upon them. The original refusal of complete participation was reversed.

This situation was greatly exacerbated by the diffusion of Nazi racial propaganda, both directly and through news reporting which quickly spread the idea that "Aryan" and "non-Aryan" were terms with some sort of scientific justification for their use, that there was a scientifically established difference in kind between the Jews and their gentile fellow citizens. Americans have long been accustomed to accept unquestioningly statements which are labeled "scientific," without bothering to consult the scientists in whose name such statements are made. The pernicious nonsense of national-socialist racialism was elaborately and fully countered by properly qualified scientists, but their mass audience was chiefly those who needed no further conviction. The greater number of Americans accepted the validity of the Hitlerian dichotomy, though for many of them this "scientific" belief had no greater emotional importance than the "scientific" claims advanced for the breakfast foods and household articles they were accustomed to purchasing.

There was (and is) however an audience, of sufficient size to be alarming, for the whole battery of Nazi anti-Jewish propaganda. This audience would appear to be composed of two major groups: individual prepsychotics, eager for any social recognition of their paranoid projections, and those first- and second-generation groups who must stifle their inner doubts and questionings by the most strident antagonism to everything which can be considered un-American. The chief anti-Jewish outrages (and they have been relatively numerous) have occurred in neighborhoods where the gentile population was indifferently assimilated.

At present these outbreaks are local and sporadic; but they represent potentially the greatest threat to the American ideal of equality, and the democracy deriving therefrom. The Jews suffer under far fewer disabilities and discriminations than the Negroes and Asians, but the recent attitude toward them differs from the attitude toward Negroes and Asians (outside the South) in as much as it is not normally accompanied by conscious feelings of guilt. Whatever individual practice may be, little theoretical assent is given to claims of "white superiority" in the greater part of the United States; discrimination is not justified by ideology. There is, however, a tendency so to justify "gentile superiority" even though at present this is chiefly confined to the aptly named "lunatic fringe." [3] If there is another depression, so that individuals are faced with failure through no fault of their own, there will be ready tinder for creating scapegoats in this reservoir of ill-will; and American democracy is built so much more on

[3] Perhaps "gentile inferiority" might be a more apt phrase. Like their Nazi confreres and models, the American anti-Semites seem to feel that ninety-seven gentiles are no match for three Jews in open competition, and therefore the majority need special laws to protect them from the excessive cleverness, industry, cunning, etc., of the minority.

egalitarian practice than on deeply held ideology that its survival would be imperiled.

Justifiable apprehension of such developments has recently led many American Jews into behavior which has had as an unintended result further emphasis on the "separateness" of the Jews. They have been emotionally deeply involved in the fate of those European Jews who have survived the Nazi massacres and have wished to help them reach safer and less tragic havens. But on account of the precariousness of their own position few have dared suggest, much less press for, a revision of the American immigration laws, which would otherwise have appeared to be the logical solution; in the earlier years of this century America absorbed more than a million immigrants a year and the country is still sparsely populated. So, to salve their consciences without immediately imperiling their own positions, they have used every political device to involve the American government in the creation of a Jewish state in Palestine; and because their votes are mostly concentrated in politically strategic areas they have been able to set one party bidding against the other in promises. By these tactics they have undermined the earlier claim that the difference between the Jews and the gentiles was exclusively one of religion; they have forced on to the general public the picture of the Jews as a separate nationality, whatever their country of adoption; and they have laid themselves open to the charge of double allegiance with as much justification as it has had when leveled against those hyphenated Americans who have tried to influence the

American government in favor of their former countries.

In marked contrast to the other incompletely American groups, the contribution which American Jews have made to American culture is great. In the sciences—particularly, perhaps, social science and medicine—in the arts and in entertainment generally their role has been a major one; they are also chiefly responsible for the peculiarly American humor, ironical, satirical, and detached. Although their role in the control of the American motion-picture and broadcasting industries has generally been exaggerated (most of the film studios are owned and controlled by non-Jewish banks) their influence on the content of these media of mass communication has been very great, and they are in large part responsible for the picture of itself which America has given to the rest of the world.

The general attitude toward the other immigrants from Europe is of a different nature. Unless they were brought into the country as young children, there is little hope or expectation that they will achieve full Americanism; but their children will do so almost without question, and their incomplete Americanism is therefore considered transitional. Many of these immigrants brought with them the political ideas of Europe; and the number of votes recorded by the Socialist party has varied approximately with the proportion of first-generation Americans in the society. When national groups of first-generation Americans are concentrated in a voting area—as, for example, the Poles in Michigan, the Germans in Chicago, or the Italians in Massachussets and Connecticut—they are able to exercise important pressure on the foreign policies of the representatives and senators they elect, as far as their former countries are concerned. The foreign-language press which serves these first-generation immigrants is ingenious in presenting arguments that the interest of America is best served by following a policy which will favor the country in whose language it is written. With the drying up of immigration these hyphenated groups are steadily decreasing in importance; in the past they have been a factor making for isolationism, for abstention from action has appeared the safest way of keeping votes. Even today their influence is disproportionate to their numbers; and current American attitudes toward such countries as Poland and Germany become more understandable with a reading of the relevant foreign-language newspapers of a couple of years earlier.[k]

The influence of these numerically unimportant groups on American foreign policy is due to the fact that American policy is normally shaped by small organized minorities, though in most cases they are "invisible" minorities united by common hopes of profit. These political minorities are commonly termed "lobbies" or "pressure groups." Since politicians are members of a despised profession, and the government is considered as something alien, there is hardly ever any force of public opinion to withstand the pressure of a determined and organized minority to have laws framed in their own interest without regard to the community. Particularly flagrant examples of such minority manipulation are the "silver bloc," whose search for greater profits for a tiny group of miners (or mine shareholders) levies a permanent tax from the whole

American public and has transformed the whole political and economic development of Asia and Central America, and the "farm bloc," whose fantastic "parity" laws have raised excessively the price of food not only in America but throughout much of the world.[1] If domestic legislation against the general interest can be not only passed but kept on the statute books, without effective popular out-cry, there is little wonder that foreign policy, which touches the general voter much less closely, can be modi-fied by equally unimportant groups.

There is one major exception to the general rule of the transformation of Europeans into Americans in two gen-erations. A great many of the Irish manage to maintain, and even to exaggerate, their national characteristics, how-ever many generations they may have been in America. This would seem to be due to a combination of two cir-cumstances: the English-speaking Irish immigrant did not have to give up his language in becoming American, and therefore there was far less break between the generations than in the case of non-English-speaking immigrants; and their Catholicism prevented them from dispersing as the English and Scots did. The priests of many of the other Catholic immigrants were perforce foreign-speaking; and consequently the Irish were concentrated in Irish-Catholic neighborhoods and chiefly intermarried among them-selves. Although not localized geographically, the Irish brogue is considered almost an American dialect. Even before the Revolution the Irish were an important com-ponent of the American population; and since the days of Andrew Jackson they have played a dominant, often preponderating, role in local and city politics, and very frequently in national politics also. Although most Irish immigrants almost inevitably came from the country, Irish Americans have settled chiefly in the big cities. Besides their accent and their religion most of them have maintained and exaggerated the traditional Irish hatred of England.

Those whose Americanism is for one reason or another considered incomplete represent between a fifth and a sixth of the population of the United States.[4] The remainder, nearly a hundred million strong, are complete "hundred per cent" Americans (the common phrase is significant). In theory these hundred million are completely equal, at least in potentialities, and differences in income and deference are meant to be due to the relative success of the efforts of each individual in the competition of life. This myth is not believed in completely, except perhaps by some college professors, but it is a major factor in the social interpretation of the obviously uneven distribution of goods and services. The hierarchy is believed to be due to individual effort and initiative, tempered by luck; some people have "had a lucky break," have "had it soft," and have therefore acquired without effort what

[4] The following figures, derived from the U. S. census of 1940, are taken from Statistical Abstracts, 1945.

Negroes	12,865,518
Foreign born (European)	11,419,138
Mexicans	1,423,533
Asiatics (including Filipinos)	254,918
American Indians	333,969
Jews	4,000,000 approx.

others have failed to achieve with the greatest hard work; but since this fortune is considered due to luck, it might have happened to anybody else—to you, to me—and the most favored are not usually considered to be different in kind from the general run of Americans.

This belief in the basic equality of American citizens has been dramatically illustrated by public-opinion polls in which representative cross-sections of Americans have been asked to assign themselves to a social class; in every case about four fifths have described themselves as middle class.[5] Although objectively such self-description is almost meaningless, subjectively it is extremely revealing. It means that the objective hierarchies are considered relatively unimportant, and that most Americans designate themselves in terms of their immediate circle of competi-

[5] Typical of such polls, which have been taken intermittently over a number of years, and fuller than most, are the following figures from the *Fortune* poll of February, 1940. The first four columns show the economic classes (for whites) which are used for making up the polling sample. Since these classes are of disparate size, the total is not a simple summation of the different groups. The self-classification of Negroes is slightly puzzling; they were presumably placing themselves in the Negro community.

Actual Class by Economic Criteria

Self-Designation by Class	Prosperous	Upper Middle	Lower Middle	Poor	Negroes	Total
Upper class	23.6	7.9	4.6	4.5	16.1	7.6
Middle class	74.7	89.0	89.4	70.3	35.7	79.2
Lower class	0.3	0.6	3.1	19.1	26.2	7.9
Don't know	1.4	2.5	2.9	6.1	22.0	5.3

The small number who classify themselves as "lower class," even among the poor and the Negroes, is noteworthy.

tion (as could be expected) and not in terms of a nation-wide hierarchy. In so far as social position is determined by income—and it is very largely—most Americans are conscious that some of their fellow citizens are worse off than they are, some better off; less than one in twelve consider that they are at the lower end of any hierarchy. Even on a national scale this concept is maintained; with typical American euphemism, people with very little money or very few goods are not nowadays described as "poor" but, at least by social workers and politicians, as "underprivileged." Lack of money may deny one some of the advantages and amenities which others enjoy, but this is envisaged as being due exclusively to lack of money; if luck or hard work subsequently gives one the money, then one has every right to all the advantages and amenities one chooses to purchase. Almost certainly one of the reasons for the resentment of the enlisted man against the officers in the United States forces was that the officers, merely on account of their rank, had amenities and facilities which were denied to the enlisted man. Such denial of equal access is practically never experienced by hundred per cent Americans in the United States; people are not generally considered disqualified from taking part in the best available owing to prior poverty or lack of education.

This belief in a basic equality, modified by differences in income due to industry and skill, is held unquestioningly by about seven eighths of the population of the United States, even though inspection will show that by the criteria of commensality, intermarriage and associations, they can be objectively divided into three social classes; [6] among the top 10 to 12 per cent (who, by the same criteria, can also be divided into three classes) the situation is very different and the competition for social superiority, employing other criteria to modify that of gross income, is waged with skill and acerbity. This competition is waged by women, above all married women; they impose the standards and make the decisions, and the position (in this competition) of men is determined by their mothers and wives.

This competition, like the other competitions which make up American life, is based on the assumption that other people's success threatens your relative position; and consequently the basic principle by which this competition is regulated is the exclusion of postulants by the relatively secure. "Exclusive" is the operative word by which

[6] The social stratification of American society has been most exhaustively studied and described by Professor W. Lloyd Warner and his associates in the six volumes of the Yankee City series, starting with *Social Life of a Modern Community*, Vol. I (New Haven, Yale University Press, 1941). A study based on parallel principles is *Deep South* by Allison Davis and his associates (Chicago, Chicago University Press, 1941). These studies established empirically the existence of six social classes in the communities observed. Although there is some difference in the personnel, the top three classes of Warner's analysis—upper upper, lower upper, upper middle—correspond fairly closely with the economic criterion of "Prosperous" used by *Fortune* in its public-opinion polls (see p. 212); and there is a similar correlation between Warner's bottom three classes—lower middle, upper lower, and lower lower, and the three *Fortune* categories of "Upper Middle," "Lower Middle," and "Poor." Warner's analysis is more exact, since the economic standards are modified by the other criteria. For elaboration of the implications of American social class, see especially John Dollard's *Caste and Class in a Southern Town* (New Haven, Yale University Press, 1937) and Margaret Mead, *op. cit.*, Chapter IV.

socially desirable position and associations are defined; and although this word has been cheapened in advertisements until it means little more than "expensive," in noncommercial usage it is still the signal which indicates areas of social competition.

These areas of social competition are circumscribed by the fact that common American practice demands equal access for everybody to anything which is paid for. In New York and its satellite resorts there are a very few "exclusive" restaurants or hotels which will turn away unknown clients, whatever their wealth; but these are not found elsewhere.

The chief area in which the battle for social position is fought are the clubs and associations for married women. In most localities the Garden Club and the Junior League are among the more important semipublic associations, membership in which is sought, as a mark of social distinction, by the newly arrived or the newly rich, and which is granted grudgingly and after the most detailed investigation by the incumbents; beyond these are the less conspicuous clubs and groups which meet at regular intervals for some specific purpose—to play bridge or music, to sew or discuss papers written by one another, to eat or to arrange flowers, or for any other pursuit suitable for leisured and cultivated women. Among the top 2 or 3 per cent of the female population of any locality membership in such small clubs and groups determines relative social position very exactly; a vast amount of diligent intrigue is put forward to secure such membership, and great heartburning and distress are felt when such intrigue is met by exclusion.

The criteria on which applicants are judged vary with the locality. In the South and in New England ancestry is the most important; descent, through as many lines as possible, from people who had positions of wealth and influence in the eighteenth or early nineteenth centuries in America overrides nearly all other considerations. Such honored ancestors are inevitably predominantly English by birth or descent. Since in such social pedigrees descent is counted bilaterally—a phenomenon not duplicated in Europe—people may have anything from one to sixteen desirable great-great-grandparents, and very subtle gradations are possible on the score of ancestry alone. In New England the sect is also indicative and the university attended by the male relatives. In the South ancestry can also score negatively: a forebear from outside the Confederate States (at least since 1865) can cancel out the merits of a number of other ancestral lines. In the rest of the country ancestry is relatively less important, and the chief criterion is descent from a family which was in the early days, even if not today, in a position of influence and affluence. Whatever the criteria used, there will be found in each community a small group of women whose dominant position is generally conceded, and who represent a court of appeal by whom applicants will be judged and included —or excluded.

This competition for social success takes up so much of the time and energy of the more prosperous and distinguished American women that it would be easy to draw the conclusion that American society—at least the top 10 per cent—has a hierarchical structure similar to that found in Western Europe in those countries which have not had a recent revolution. But the differences are far greater than the surface similarity. Most important is the fact that these hierarchies are local, and not nation-wide. The criteria which grant top position in South Carolina are not admitted in Vermont or Wyoming, and conversely. The attention paid to the ramifications of kinship may be of some aid to the well-connected in establishing themselves in a new community, but such aid is neither important nor sure. There is a volume called *The New York Social Register* which attempts to list the distinguished of the whole country (applicants for inclusion must present letters from two *women* whose husbands or sons are already included); but although the number included is small, the doyennes of each community will consider some inclusions unjustified, as well as some exclusions. With this partial exception, competition for social success, like competition for business success, is predominantly one for relative position in a group of near equals; it is not validating an absolute position by the display of behavior appropriate to that position.

The impact of this competition for social position is further diminished by the fact that social position is determined by women, and the economic and political structures of the United States are still patriarchal in form. In consequence, considerations of family and social precedence have very little weight in determining which men will fill which positions. Men are involved as husbands and sons in the mixed entertainments by which women validate their relative social positions; but since invitations are given and accepted in this group without in many cases primary consideration being given to the economic or political positions of the attached males, such associations are seldom influential in the public career of the men involved. The one major exception to this generalization occurs when a young man of low social and economic position marries the daughter of parents of higher status; in such a case the man gets assimilated to his wife's position and may reap considerable benefit therefrom. In the reverse situation the wife from a lower social class will have a harder time in acquiring membership in the important small clubs other than those in which her husband's mother and sisters are members.

In short, in the upper tenth of fully American society relative position is of great emotional importance, the cause of many humiliations and sadistic triumphs, but with little social impact. The claims to special distinction advanced by the upper tenth are somewhat resented by the rest of the population; but they accept the standards of behavior which would have to serve them as models if they "made good." Variations in income have an obvious determining influence on the differential distribution of all the goods within the society, education and medical attention, houses and food; and where the contrast is great the experiences which shape character and the goals considered desirable may vary consistently, so that slightly different emphases may be discovered at different social and economic levels. In the top 10 per cent who are economically secure, relative position is determined by secondary considerations; but these are not important enough to out-

weigh the basic belief that all full Americans are fundamentally equal, and that the differences between them are
due to the differences in individual ability, industry, and
luck. Needless to say, all full Americans are considered
naturally superior to all whose Americanism is incomplete,
for Americanism is an act of will.

Note, 1963. Although the changing situation and condition of American Negroes are now in the forefront of
worldwide attention, I have not thought it necessary or
desirable to modify this chapter. The generalizations
made on pp. 196–199 still seem to me valid; and I have
no recent personal experience or sources of information
which would enable me to re-interpret or add to the stories which fill the news media of every country in the
world. For the present involvement of young white Americans in the issue, see Postscript p. 263.

ᵏ These hyphenated groups today are probably influential in keeping
up the clamor to "liberate" the countries of Eastern Europe from their
communist governments.

¹ The laws and regulations concerning oil-depletion allowances are
relevant in this context.

IX

LESSER BREEDS

The belief that Americanism can be more or less complete, and that this relative completeness is above all a matter of will, is a most important component in the attitude of most Americans toward the inhabitants of the rest of the world. Viewed from one aspect, all the people, and all the peoples, of the world can be placed at different positions along a single continuum, with one hundred per cent Americanism at the positive end, and what might be called one hundred per cent un-Americanism at the negative. Such a schematic concept is not, as far as I know, consciously formulated by any group in the United States; but the speeches and actions of Americans of every political persuasion become far more comprehensible if they are interpreted in the light of such an unformulated scale. Since full Americanism and full humanity are equated, peoples who are placed on the negative half of the continuum—as, for example, the Japanese during the last war—are denied human status and forfeit human rights.[m] Until surrender and the consequent occupation transformed the Japanese into postulant Americans, Americans from the forces would recount to their approving compatriots tales of cruelty and deception practiced on the Japanese soldiers which would almost certainly have evoked disapproval if animals had been involved instead.

For European peoples the criteria for approximation to Americanism are much the same as for European immigrants, except that housing amenities and public services take on considerably more importance as indicative symptoms; further criteria are the degree of technological development and the political forms. Political forms are judged quite simply by their resemblance to or difference from American forms. Thus a republic is better than a monarchy, two parties are better than one or three, the separation of church and state is better than their amalgamation, a president is better than a king or a dictator, a separate judiciary is better than a subordinate judiciary, two houses of elected representatives are better than one or three, the absence of hereditary titles is better than their presence. To the degree that political forms of a foreign country correspond to those of the United States, to that degree, other things being equal, is that country considered to approximate to Americanism. But when this political aspect is being considered, a synonym for Americanism is habitually used: the synonym is "democracy."

This synonym has been established by the simplest of syllogisms: American political forms are democratic, therefore political forms which are like those of America are like democracy. This syllogism is unquestioned by the overwhelming majority of Americans: were Sweden or Greece to abolish their monarchies without otherwise changing in any respect their political behavior they would be considered to have become far more democratic by so doing. And conversely, no matter how complete the social security or the political equality of the British, they will be considered incompletely democratic while they retain the monarchy and hereditary titles.[1]

For the vast majority of Americans the term "democracy" has no connotations beyond "political forms after the American fashion." Those propagandists, paid or amateur, who wish to convince the American public that the political regimes of such countries as Italy or Yugoslavia are worthy of support do so by pointing out how much nearer their present forms are to the American model compared with those they have replaced. Indeed partisans of all foreign countries use the same principle for commendation, telling Americans that the country they are advocating resembles, or aspires to resemble, America. This technique has probably been carried to its furthest pitch by naïve and well-meaning advocates of international co-operation like the late Wendell Willkie and Henry Wallace [2] who have claimed, with apparently no feeling of incongruity, that conditions in Siberia or in

[1] Until very recently Americans from the middle and upper classes combined with their sense of superiority to the European immigrants a feeling of uncomfortable inferiority toward members of the European intellectual and social elites (see Mead, *op. cit.*, Chapter V).

[2] See Wendell Willkie, *One World* (New York, Simon and Schuster, 1943) and Henry Wallace *passim*, but especially the speeches he made during and after his journey through Siberia and China in May, June, and July, 1944. In Chungking he said: "Some American has said that Americans are fighting for the right to throw pop bottles at the umpire in Brooklyn. That's one way of looking at it. We're fighting for our way of life. That doesn't mean we are trying to make the rest of the world like America—plumbing isn't everything. But we can hope the rest of the world will come to like many of our ways and adopt them."

Yunnan are strictly parallel with those on the American frontier a century ago.

For those countries in which the people's appearance, clothes, food, housing amenities, and political forms are completely different from those of Americans, above all the countries of Asia, the best means by which their inhabitants can be presented as tending toward Americanism, and therefore meriting treatment as human beings, is by describing their character as typically American. In recent years the Chinese have been the special recipients of this peculiar form of flattery; judging by the majority of books and speeches on that country one would imagine that only the most superficial differences distinguished the valley of the Yangtze from that of the Mississippi.[3] But though the Chinese are particularly favored in this respect, there is no country in Asia, no matter how hierarchic its structure, how absolute its government, how priest-ridden its people, how otherworldly its aims, which has not had its advocates explaining that its inhabitants are "really" just like Americans.

If public sympathy for, or support of, a foreign people is desirable, it is essential that such an identification be made. Unless this minimum of Americanism is ascribed to them, how can they be considered human at all? And

[3] The chief impetus to this consideration of the Chinese as American characters with Oriental habits probably arose from the great popular success of the novels of Pearl Buck. Her best-selling trilogy, *House of Earth* (New York and London, 1931), portrayed the economic and social rise of a Chinese family through the exercise of private enterprise, and its subsequent disintegration in terms with which American readers could identify themselves with the greatest of ease. The fact that the initial "break" was a theft did not prevent this.

if they are not human, they are things: and things cannot be sympathized with or supported, they can only be exploited or destroyed.

It is in good part due to this widely held and basic attitude that foreigners are only worthy of respect and consideration in so far as they approximate to Americanism, that American advocates of international co-operation act as if they felt themselves forced to present a grossly distorted picture of the rest of the world to their own compatriots. Apparently to persuade Americans that war between their country and the U. S. S. R. would be disastrous many "liberals" feel it to be necessary to paint a completely unrealistic picture of Russian society as practically identical with that of America except for a few technological developments; to admit that Soviet society is markedly different in form and in values from American society is willfully to imperil the peace. As a consequence the "liberal" newspapers and books of contemporary America, despite their undoubted good intentions, are in general far less accurate and trustworthy, as far as foreign affairs are concerned, than those which can rightly be dubbed "conservative." For the internationalists, far more than for the isolationists, the "one-ness" of the world is a universal Americanism.

It is this attitude, too, which gives an idiosyncratic aspect to American co-operation in international undertakings. For most Americans, particularly in situations where the political aspect is not prominent, taking part in an international undertaking means extending American activities outside the boundaries of the United States.

They will give their time, their skill, and their resources with great generosity and without afterthought; but it is most difficult for them to concede the desirability of forms of organization other than those they are used to, or to take into account values, preferences, or prejudices which they have not encountered inside the United States. The belief in the universal aspiration toward Americanism is so pervasive that it is abandoned with the greatest difficulty; and when circumstances force its abandonment, international co-operation is liable to be abandoned, too. People so perverse as to choose to remain foreign deserve no help.

Men of good will can maintain for a long time their belief in the universal aspiration toward Americanism by stressing the distinction between peoples and their governments. With practically no exceptions, Americans regard their own government as alien; they do not identify themselves with it, do not consider themselves involved in its actions, feel free to criticize and despise it. This is most clearly demonstrated when Americans discuss American policies or activities abroad; it is "they" who have made this policy, taken this move, written this note—never "we." This detached attitude is shared even by most of the members of Congress and the American civil service who are not personally involved in a given activity or foreign policy; there is no feeling of joint responsibility or indirect participation.

This almost universal consideration of the government as alien and its personnel as tainted with the lust for authority and unworthy of respect has regular repercussions on American foreign policy. These attitudes affect the people who should devise and carry out the policies; they realize they are suspect and are therefore exaggeratedly frightened of public criticism; policies which officials are convinced would be desirable are not even mooted in public from fear of offending public opinion. Because the government is despised and suspect, Congress will only allow quite inadequate salaries to be paid to civil servants; since the symbolic value of a high income is so great, and since being in government is a low-regarded profession, the more able civil servants are constantly being lured away by offers of better paid and more respected posts in business or the professions. This constant draining away of the more able people has as a first result a lack of continuity of personnel, and so often a lack of continuity of policy; a second result is that the people who resist the offers of business and remain in the State Department or foreign service tend to be people who do not fully share the general American attitude toward authority; and public suspicion of the State Department maintains that its personnel is unduly biased in favor of the two arch-symbols of authority—England and the Roman Catholic Church.

The general lack of identification with the government is most exaggerated among intellectuals. When they discuss foreign affairs this detachment becomes positively Olympian; the rejection of any responsibility for, or participation in, the activities of their own government gives them, it would seem, special qualifications for telling other governments how they should act.

This distinction between peoples and their governments which Americans feel so intimately is regularly
ascribed to foreign peoples with whom friendly relations
are desired but whose political forms differ markedly from
the American pattern. Thus, in face of all the available
evidence, interested Americans insisted both during and
after the recent war that the German people were predominantly hostile to national socialism and Hitler; and other
interested groups are stressing with equal vehemence today the distinction between the "common" Russian and
his government. This belief can be maintained even after
considerable personal contact with nationals of the relevant countries; for, since full Americanism and full humanity are equated, the more human foreigners are shown
to be on further acquaintance, the more American they
can be presumed to be in character.

Since Americans so regularly fail to identify themselves
with their own government, and since they generally ascribe a similar failure to foreigners, American international relations tend to assume the same forms as American interpersonal relations. The diverse components
which make up the relationships between Americans and
their fellows are all present in the attitudes and demands
of Americans in their relations with foreign peoples; since
now one aspect, now another, comes to the fore, there are
considerable apparent alternations and internal contradictions in the attitudes of Americans toward a given country
over a stretch of time.

One of the most important and constant components of
such relations is the insatiable American demand for the

signs of friendship and love. Part of my duties during the war was the reading of a large number of technical descriptions, prepared by different American government agencies, of various remote countries and peoples in Asia, Africa, and Oceania. In every one of these reports, no matter how technical the greater part of the subject matter, there was a paragraph on the attitudes of the natives toward the principal Occidental countries, and, without exception, these paragraphs stated that of all foreign countries America was the most loved, the most admired, the most trusted. It didn't matter how small and obscure the peoples were, how little experience they had had of Americans, or even, as in the case of some Micronesian islands, if they had had none at all within living memory, this paragraph asserting that the natives loved, admired, and trusted America above all other countries had to find a place. To read of a people to whom such sentiments were not ascribed would, it would appear, be as damaging to one's self-esteem as to be faced with an unsmiling shoeshine boy or a silent bartender. In this context it is necessary to recall the nonsymmetrical aspect of love in America: to be loved it is not necessary to love in return, but rather to be worthy of love. In the documents referred to there was no suggestion that this aboriginal love and admiration were reciprocated.

Love between peoples, strictly analogous to the love between individuals, is felt by many Americans to be of major importance in determining whether there shall be peace or war between America and the country under discussion. And so Americans of good will are constantly putting forward plans to assure world peace by bringing over large groups of individuals (usually students) from countries felt to be hostile to the United States. If twenty thousand Russians (for example) came over annually to spend two years in American colleges, they would return so filled with love and admiration that war between the two countries would be impossible. Sometimes these good-will visits are envisaged on a reciprocal basis, though this is much less common; America does not love Bulgaria (say) enough, because not enough Americans know enough Bulgarians; if two hundred Americans go into as many Bulgarian homes, American-Bulgar relations will be perceptibly improved. But this symmetrical view is rare: generally it is thought that America will show herself worthy of love by good works—schools, hospitals, dispensaries, missions, technical know-how; the foreigners will give their love when their ignorance of America's worthiness has been dispelled.

This belief in love as a major factor in international relations has a number of consequences, of which the most important is the consistent underestimation of the "impersonal" components of such relations, such as economic and ideological considerations. Secondly, this belief engenders an excessive sensitivity to the changing attitudes of foreign countries or those who are believed to be their representatives or spokesmen; there are constant articles in the press rating America's popularity in different parts of the world, and a reported lessening of popularity is considered both a danger to peace and a personal rejection. It is therefore particularly difficult for America to carry through a long-term policy which demands initial unpopular measures. The "tough" treatments originally proposed for the conquered populations of Germany and Japan made almost intolerably difficult psychological demands on the Americans designated to be the agents of those policies; to live surrounded by people who manifestly didn't love one, and whom one was forbidden to woo with gifts of food and cigarettes, with assistance and simple friendliness, with the nearest possible approach to "dating," would be too painful for well-adjusted Americans for any length of time. The nonfraternization orders showed as little understanding of American psychology as did the eighteenth amendment enforcing prohibition; and, like that well-intentioned law, they were disobeyed with added zest. If Americans are placed in a situation where they feel they are not loved their natural tendency is to withdraw, physically if possible; if that is not possible, then chemically, through alcohol, or ideologically, into isolation.

Coupled with this desire to be loved is a strong fear of rejection, of being treated as unworthy of love; and one technique of dealing with this fear is to anticipate it, by rejecting before one is rejected. This is one more component making for isolationism, in addition to the deep emotional rejection of Europe already described, and the fear of losing the votes of local ethnic groups, a reproduction on an international scale of the response "Let's get the hell out of here" which is a well-worn individual technique for dealing with uncomfortable situations. Papers and propagandists who advocate isolationism as a consistent policy hope to win converts by reminding their readers and listeners how America has been rejected in the past, been called "Uncle Sham" or "Uncle Shylock"; such past rejection is advanced as sufficient reason for avoiding rejection in the future.

This fear of rejection has, as it were, an obverse side—the fear of being exploited, of being made a sucker of, of not being truly loved for oneself alone but only for what one provides, the fear of being considered "Uncle Santa." This is the meanest as well as one of the most prevalent American fears, and the one most likely to damage international relations, now that America is the universal creditor. Coupled with this fear of being "had," there are nearly always statements about American inferiority in international dealings; foreign countries are too cunning, too persuasive in their propaganda, too apt at flattering the naïve American representatives for it to be safe for America to treat with them. In this picture, which is the one predominantly presented by the isolationist press, the feminine identification of America is almost undisguised: America is pictured as the naïve and beautiful farmer's daughter, whose simple virtue is in constant danger from the wicked fascinations of the city slickers. In such cases the desire to be loved is overpowered by the fear of being seduced and abandoned.

The demand for love and the hurt pain when love is refused color many American responses to international situations. Thus, a very important component in the current general attitudes toward Soviet Russia and Yugoslavia springs from what is felt to be the ingratitude of these countries in the face of American benevolence. America gave lend-lease supplies, voted the greater part of the money for U. N. R. R. A., which did much for the victory and rehabilitation of these countries. Instead of receiving thanks and love, the American representative in Moscow had to extort a grudging acknowledgment of the gifts, the Russian newspapers were filled with abuse of their benefactor, the Yugoslavs shot down their planes. Benevolence earned, not love, but abuse and rejection; each such experience gave added weight to the arguments of the isolationists and weakened the position of the advocates of international co-operation.

The demand for the signs of friendship and love is only one of the components of the relations between Americans. A second is the competition for relative success. In the international sphere, however, the analogy is less the competition between individuals than the competition between business concerns, at least in the minds of those directly or indirectly involved in international economic transactions. America is, as it were, envisaged as a large corporation engaged in an endless competition for markets and profits with the other corporations who are the remaining national states of the world. In such dealings any considerations other than the expansion and profit of one's own corporation are irrelevant. The rules governing such commercial competition should ideally be those of unrestricted "free enterprise"; if these are, regrettably, modified, every effort must be made to see that your competitors do not gain an unfair advantage over you. It is unfair if they pay their workers less than you do, and such discrepancies should be made good by tariffs; it is unfair if two of your competitors enter into a mutual contract from which you are excluded, and attempts are made to prevent this by the international equivalents of antitrust laws; it is unfair if foreign corporations try to invade your territory, and it is equally unfair if foreign corporations try to exclude you from their territory. As a business concern, a corporation's sole object and justification is to show increasing and continuous profits for its shareholders (or citizens); it should buy in the cheapest market and sell in the dearest; if in the course of these transactions other firms go bankrupt and cannot continue in business, what concern is it of ours? What do you think we're in this for? Our health?

The parallel between the national state as an economic unit and the private trading corporation is pushed as far as it will go by the "hardheaded" American businessman, often with results which threaten world disaster. Within a single economy it is possible to drive competitors into bankruptcy and ruin without affecting in any way the stability of the economy as a whole, whatever individual misery may be caused; but a bankrupt state cannot be similarly absorbed. In the business world no quarter is given, and none is asked, and it is generally believed that the community as a whole is benefited thereby. No similar claim can rightly be made when such behavior is projected onto the world scene. But when a situation is defined as "business" an American cannot act with self-approval, much less receive the approval and consent of his fellows, unless he follows the principles which hold good for private trading. "The business of America is business."

Political alliances are envisaged as similar to combinations between corporations in which two (or more) companies will pool their resources and co-ordinate their policies to dispose of a rival. Once the rival has been disposed of, the association, which was strictly *ad hoc*, is automatically at an end; both have been benefited by the removal of the rival from the field, and now can revert to mutual competition under the rules of free enterprise which is the proper normal state of healthy corporations. Since the shared activity was mutually profitable it entails no further obligations on the formerly contracted parties.

The violent contrasts between Americans acting as hardheaded businessmen and as kind simple guys who just want to be liked are the cause of the greatest amount of the confusion and distrust with which the foreign activities of the United States are viewed by non-Americans. Americans are generally not conscious of the contrast because, as has been pointed out, they tend to view each situation separately, as it were atomically; if a situation is defined as one of business, one type of conduct is appropriate; if defined as one of human relations, a quite different type of conduct is called for, just as you treat a business rival differently in his office or at the country club. The drawback to this analogy in international relations is that non-Americans seldom share this custom of defining appropriate behavior in terms of the immediate context only, and may well give different definitions to the situations from those adopted by Americans.

A further cause of confusion is that Americans not only switch continuously from the role of the businessman to the role of the kind simple guy, they also speak sometimes with the voice of Uncle Sam, sometimes with that of the Goddess of Liberty. The Goddess of Liberty, the encapsulated mother and schoolmarm, speaks in terms of moral imperatives and prohibitions; she tells the world what it should do and should not do, when it should fight and when it should kiss and make up, when it should give some of its candy to the other children, and when it should stand up for itself and not let itself be put upon. The Goddess of Liberty, as has already been said, lays down these rules of conduct for others with complacent assurance that she is right, but she does not feel they apply to herself; a mother or schoolmistress is not supposed to act in the same way as the boys she is rearing. To people who have not been reared in the same way it is often disconcerting when the voice of the schoolmistress comes out of the mouth of a senator or newspaper columnist; and those who do not envisage Morality as a Goddess, debarred by her status from taking part in many of the activities she prescribes, mistakenly interpret such injunctions as hypocritical.

The attitudes so far discussed are those of the general run of Americans with no deep emotional involvement with any particular foreign country. There is, however, also an important minority of Americans who become emotionally most deeply involved with specific foreign countries. Such involvement would appear to be due to variations of individual history or personality, and to take two main forms.

The first of these consists in the subvention of revolutions abroad. Many of the revolutions of this century, particularly those aiming at the establishment of the political independence of peoples formerly dependent, have been made possible in great part by American gifts of money. The cases of Czechoslovakia and Ireland are well-established examples; traces of similar activities can be seen in the recent situations in Palestine, Poland, and Greece. It has been suggested to me that these activities are supported predominantly by second-generation Americans whose fathers came from the countries concerned, and that the gifts are attempts to atone for the rejection of their fathers and their countries, countries which in most cases they have no desire to visit, and whose tongue they are unable to speak. It is ironical that citizens of a country so politically conservative and so apprehensive of domestic revolution that any proposed change can be damned in the eyes of the majority by labeling it "communist" should so often be the mainsprings of revolution and terrorism abroad.

Other Americans, with no such genealogical connections with specific foreign countries, also become deeply involved in the fortunes of particular countries, or of political parties therein. These would appear to be people whose emotional needs do not find sufficient scope in their immediate environment and who search the world for a larger screen on which to project their feelings of oppression and injustice, of being insufficiently loved and respected. In this case there are nearly always two concomitant psychological features: the individual Americans identify themselves very deeply with the inhabitants of the country they are interested in, and they become fiercely partisan. This partisanship overrides all other considerations. Americans who have chosen Poland, or Yugoslavia, or China (to take current examples) on which to project their own unconscious hopes or fears will only accept news or countenance policies which favor the group they have chosen; even within the government it is rare to find an American whose first consideration is the interest of the United States in regard to (say) Yugoslavia or China; they are for or against Marshal Tito, for or against Chiang Kai-shek; they try to influence public opinion and the actions of the United States government in favor of the side they have adopted and to persuade the indifferent world that morality and democracy are served thereby. The interest of their own country is rarely considered by such passionate partisans; the normal American failure to identify with the government is in such people enhanced, until the American government becomes an enemy to be tricked and outwitted in favor of a party in a foreign country which its proponents may well have never visited and of whom all their knowledge is second- or third-hand.

When normally well-adjusted Americans are made aware of the political situation in any foreign country their habitual reaction is to divide the inhabitants into oppressors and oppressed, and side with the latter. The rejection of authority is so fundamental that the belief that another group is trying to reject authority is a sure ground for sympathy and for a measure of identification, however inhuman the "underdogs" may be in all other respects. The general American concern about India (and to a certain extent all dependent peoples outside the Western Hemisphere) is founded on the "American," and so "democratic," implications of resistance to authority. To be against authority is to be worthy of sympathy and help. Emotionally, India in recent years has been seen as resembling America in 1775; outside the realm of emotion the parallel is nearly meaningless. But for most Americans the internal affairs of other countries are only of interest from the emotional point of view; spontaneously and generously, though often unthinkingly and irrationally, they take the part of the underdog as their own. To maintain this identification the underdogs must stand up for themselves; underdogs who appear to acquiesce in their position quickly arouse American discomfort and eventually rejection.

In the case of the passionate partisans this typical American attitude is frequently reversed, and the powerful and authoritarian are identified with because they are powerful and authoritarian, because through them the partisan can vicariously gratify desires which cannot be gratified directly within the political framework of the United States. This attitude was most clearly crystallized in Anne Morrow Lindbergh's *Wave of the Future*, of which the fundamental argument was that Americans should give support to national socialism and fascism because they were powerful, and were going to become more powerful. Today the powerful are given the veneer of respectability by being considered "anti-communist"; and some Americans will passionately defend repressive regimes from Spain or Portugal to Taiwan because these are "strong" governments with "strong" men at their head. The arguments which were advanced before 1941 for supporting national socialism and fascism are repeated today with only minimal verbal changes and often by the same persons. Spokesmen who deplore and resist every extension of the power of their own government applaud and support the most powerful governments overseas, undisturbed by any feeling of inconsistency. For such people, power is to be admired, provided they are not personally incommoded by the power of others.

Apart from these furtive worshipers of power, American partisanship is most generally manifested toward Asian countries and political groups therein. The attitude of the majority of educated Americans toward Asia is different in kind and degree from their attitudes toward the rest of the world. Asia is the one continent about which Americans are emotionally detached. Europe is the repudiated and rejected land of their forefathers; the physical appearance of the Africans revives feelings of guilt and distaste; Latin America is a sort of despised strategic hinterland, to be protected from European encroachments, faintly ridiculous with its endless political upheavals, backward and unsanitary even if picturesque, inhabited by amorous, lazy, and untrustworthy "Latins" whom it is politic to patronize but impossible to admire.

With the intermittent exception of Japan, Asians are

more separate from Americans, both physically and emotionally, than any other peoples. An Asian appearance evokes far fewer memories than does a Caucasian or Negroid; Asians are not threatening (they are physically smaller) nor are they distasteful parodies. They are most of them politically oppressed and can therefore be sympathized and identified with as underdogs, as well as providing vicarious atonement for the treatment of the American Negroes; and an American hostility to the government can generally be imputed to those whose government is not alien.

A kindly and generally unpatronizing interest in Asians is therefore felt by most educated Americans, manifested in the generous support given to medical and religious missionaries, and by other tangible and material aids: politically Americans like to think of themselves as patrons and protectors of the peoples of Asia against the depredations and exploitations of the rest of the world. This is the general attitude; but in a considerable number of individual cases identification with the fate of an Asian political group is carried up to and beyond fanaticism.

The American partisans of Asians from Haifa to Hong Kong are above all things dedicated to freeing their adopted peoples from the depredations and exploitations of the British. For the majority of Americans there only exists one empire in the world, the British Empire. Although specialists in the region are intellectually aware that France and the Netherlands control (or controlled till recently) considerable populations in Asia, this is a fact of little emotional importance, and it would be hard to find passionate American advocates of any long standing for the independence of French Indo-China or the Dutch East Indies. The existence of the American Empire is simply denied emotionally and intellectually, and few well-informed Americans could make even a rough estimate of its population, a moderately complete list of the "Dependencies" and "Possessions" of which it is composed, or say how any portions of it are governed. If pressed, they would probably (and incorrectly) assume that it was governed democratically; [4] but few Americans have any doubt as to how the British Empire is run; it is run completely despotically and autocratically, the exemplar of authority at its most unbridled and arbitrary.

This belief in the unparalleled iniquity of the British Empire is held unquestioningly by the vast majority of Americans, even by those who admire and love England. The picture is painted in the history books from the first grade onward; the British Empire of today is conceived as an unmodified extension of the British Empire of 1775, of George III and Lord North. The moral of the textbooks is never seriously questioned; the British Empire is evil and oppressive, and anybody helping to weaken or overthrow it is helping the cause of democracy, truth, and justice. The fact that victory over Japan was completely dependent on dominion and empire bases has only been realized by professional strategists; whatever the longer-term

[4] Except for the Philippines, no portion of the American Empire elects the representatives who frame the laws and impose the taxes. The empire is administered in part by the Department of the Interior (!) and in part by the Navy Department. The populations dependent on the latter enjoy the minimum of civil rights.

consequences American opinion can always be split by calling attention to the existence of the empire.

The unique wickedness of the empire is one of the components in the complex of American attitudes toward Britain. Together with this wanton authority there often goes a belief in the unparalleled cunning, unscrupulousness, deviousness, subtlety of propaganda, and general Machiavellism of the British which, on suitable ground, can produce fine full-blown paranoid constructions. Even in well-balanced Americans these beliefs are latent; and in Washington I was often surprised at the ingenious and subtle explanations devised by my American colleagues for Britain's blunders and stupidities: they found it as difficult to believe that the British could be inefficient on a political level as to credit them with efficiency on a mechanical one.

Although the attributes commonly ascribed to the British are morally deplorable, they cannot be treated with the indifference suitable to the morally deplorable attributes of continental Europeans. For one thing, they imply a sort of superiority, which even if disapproved of offers a challenge of a different nature to European immoralities.[5] But more important is the fact that most Americans share with most Englishmen the belief that the United States has been predominantly peopled by English stock.

---

[5] An extremely widespread misconception about Britain held by a great number of Americans concerns the size of its population. The general belief is that it is only slightly smaller than that of the United States. I have found that highly respected and influential political commentators believe that the population of the British Isles is somewhere between eighty and a hundred million.

This is a purely mythical belief. Before the Revolution the English and their descendants were the largest group in the country and at that period they held all the chief positions of power and influence; the Founding Fathers were predominantly English in education and character.[*] However, since the great immigrations which started in 1870 the English have become a relatively unimportant component in the amalgam of the Melting Pot. Owing to intermarriage it is impossible to calculate with any accuracy the proportions in which the various European stocks are represented among contemporary Americans; but intelligent guesses estimate that the descendants of the Irish or of the Germans both approach in number the descendants of the English, and together outnumber the latter; and this takes no account of the descendants of all the other European stocks. Today the descendants of the English are at most the largest single ethnic minority within the country.

Though a belief may be unfounded in historical fact it can nevertheless be psychologically potent; and the general American belief that most other Americans are descended from the English has had an important influence on American attitudes toward England. As has already been noted, the upper class along the Atlantic seaboard place great emphasis on their English ancestry; as a consequence the English are to a large extent identified as upper class, and receive much of the resentment which

[*] Benjamin Franklin and Patrick Henry would seem to have had American characters; but most of the other Founding Fathers can be imagined more easily in contemporary England than in the contemporary United States.

cannot be so safely directed at the socially prominent. This belief is kept vivid by the stereotyped picture of the Englishman in radio, film, and cartoon (the titled, monocled, tea-drinking, haw-hawing nitwit who aspires to and often succeeds in marrying the rich heiress); by the great emphasis given to the British royal family in all the press, and to the existence of the aristocracy in the isolationist papers; and by the fact that visiting Englishmen tend to appear prominently and consistently in the society pages of local papers. Even through its casual visitors, England tends to be identified with authority.

Most Americans feel toward England as though it were an authoritarian father—wicked, past its prime, old-fashioned, passed and left behind, but still a father; they can never be indifferent to Britain as they can to the rest of the world. They are more sensitive toward Britain, more conscious of its faults and failings, than they are in the case of any other country, just as one is more sensitive to the public behavior of relations than to that of strangers. Many Americans have an ideal of the line of conduct which Britain should pursue which is far higher than that demanded of any other people, or of themselves; that, too, is compatible with the image. Until recently, and for many Americans even today, there have been no limits imagined to England's strength; refusal to take aggressive action, whether in Manchuria, at Munich or in Palestine, has consistently been ascribed to wickedness, never to weakness; England could right what was wrong in the rest of the world, and its refusal to do so was perverse. Even the British demand for a loan, following the impoverishment of two wars, was felt to be like an improvident parent in his old age demanding support from his despised but capable son; and the loan was granted with that mixture of revenge and grudging annoyance which would be appropriate in such family circumstances. In 1843 Dickens heard England referred to as that "unnat'ral old parent"; a century has not fundamentally changed that attitude.

In one way England may be said to be part of the American character, to be one aspect of the authoritarian father which has been incorporated. In nearly every individual case the actual fathers have been rejected, together with the countries from which they or their ancestors came; the few father-figures on the internal scene are mostly feared and resented; but on the fringe of consciousness there remains England as an image of an authoritarian father— hated and loved, feared and admired, resented and copied, mistrusted and relied on, despised and looked up to, regarded with a sensitive ambivalence which can never sink to indifference.

During nearly two centuries men, women, and children have abandoned their homes and countries and crossed the oceans to the United States of North America, carrying with them the hope of finding there some freedom or opportunity that their country of birth could not or did not give them. They made the journey as individuals, at most as small families, united only negatively by their rejection of the countries they had left behind. The original settlement, made by loyal Englishmen and by Englishmen who had rejected English tyranny, succeeded in unparalleled fashion in assimilating these millions from all over the world, giving their children a common American character and unwittingly, almost inadvertently, forming a nation. The advance of democracy in the old world involved the lessening of the rights of the state and the increase in the rights of the individual. Uniquely, America did not start as a state, but as millions of individuals seeking their own advantage. The peril of the old world is, and always has been, tyranny; the peril of the new world is anarchy. The bounty of nature, the fortunes of war, and the drive and know-how of individuals have made the United States already the richest country in the world and potentially the strongest; if to these qualities are added general civic responsibility and political farsightedness its power and influence will be incalculable.

---

[m] It is a curious reflection that, although this chapter was written in 1947, and reflected the political attitudes of that time, the major alteration which would need to be made today is the replacing of "Japanese" by "Chinese" throughout, and *vice versa*. The Japanese are now completely rehabilitated, their art and their religion worthy of imitation, their politics fully "democratic"; whereas the Chinese of Communist China are practically deprived of human status. Otherwise humane people have treated reports of famine and starvation in Communist China as a cause for rejoicing; and suggestions that the United States might help in alleviating such human misery have been regarded as treachery.

POSTSCRIPT, 1963:
FOREIGN MATTER

THE VISIBLE, physical changes are immediately striking; the centers of many cities in the United States have been far more radically reconstructed and rebuilt than have the most completely war-devastated towns of Europe that I know. As an example of this destruction and reconstruction, I may cite the fact that of all the hotels and apartment houses which I had lived in between 1935 and 1950, only two remained standing in 1963: an apartment building in New Haven and a hotel in San Francisco; all the rest—and I visited the sites of about a dozen—have completely disappeared, their places typically taken by bigger buildings in a modern idiom, office blocks rather than residences.

This physical change in the make-up of most of America's major cities has had a number of direct and indirect consequences. The most obvious, and the most frequently commented on, is the fact that the centers of most cities are abandoned after office hours and over weekends by the people who work in the offices; they are either empty (Times Square seems emptier than Piccadilly Circus after about ten-thirty in the evening) or given over to the least fortunate of the foreign-born, the Puerto Ricans, and to the poorest native-born Americans, Negro or white.[1]

As always, the foreign-born and the poor are the recipients of inadequate social and municipal services; the empty city centers tend to be indifferently policed, especially at night; the city streets, even more the city parks, are dangerous. Anybody alone and on foot runs the risk of being "mugged"—knocked unconscious, possibly more gravely hurt, and robbed. This occurs sufficiently frequently not to be newsworthy; it is not even an interesting subject of conversation, though, if the topic is raised, most people can recount an incident from among their acquaintances. Taxi drivers consider the night shift perilous.

The most usual explanation given for this increase in petty robbery with violence is that the criminals are youngsters under the influence of marijuana or more dangerous drugs, desperate for money to pay the extortionate prices which the peddlers demand and (in general belief) rendered fearless and cruel by the mysterious powers hidden in the drugs they have consumed. For the public at large the effects of marijuana are considered to be of quite a different nature from the effects of alcohol. In many circles, the drunk is looked upon with affectionate tolerance, and the alcoholic with sympathy; the personality changes produced by drink are considered normal and,

[1] See Note, page 219, for the reason why I do not discuss in detail the present condition of Negroes in this postscript.

within very wide limits, "fun"; but the personality changes produced by hemp or any of the synthetic drugs are felt to be *uncanny* and frightening. It would seem to be open to argument whether the direct effects of marijuana are more deleterious or socially undesirable than those of alcohol, were it not that its illegality drives its consumers and small-scale distributors into the criminal underworld (as did drinking during prohibition); but in the present climate of American opinion it would seem impossible to argue this dispassionately, much less conduct the controlled experiments on which alone informed opinion could be based. For the vast majority of Americans of good will, the wickedness of narcotics is not open to question. Narcotics, it is felt, change the personality in unpredictable and therefore dangerous ways, and so present a threat to the American character and the American way of life. This point of view will be sincerely advanced by people who medicate themselves with stimulants, sedatives, and tranquilizers, take their problems to be untangled by psychiatrists of any or no qualifications, and regularly drink before meals. There are, of course, two influential groups who have a considerable interest in keeping narcotics illegal: the "vice barons" and the federal narcotics squad; but the fear of narcotics on the part of the respectable would not seem to depend on propaganda from either source. It seems to be one aspect of the amorphous fear of some external foreign substance getting into one and transforming one's personality or health which perplexes and distresses so many Americans today.

This fear of contamination would seem to be very widespread among contemporary Americans, particularly those living on or near either seaboard; by contrast, the people of the Middle West seem relatively free from such anxieties, still optimistic and easy going, self-confident and generous. In many towns on the Eastern seaboard, women alone in a house or apartment are frightened about answering the doorbell. Nor is this fear unfounded; New Haven, for example, has had a series of rapes, Boston a series of stranglings in the early months of 1963; there is realistic danger.

There is also some realistic danger in all the other fears of contamination. Strontium 90 fallout from the testing of atomic weapons is an undoubted danger, and is so recognized by the American (and other) governments, who make elaborate tests of the safety level. But these tests are not convincing to some of the people most concerned with this danger, predominantly members of S A N E; and I met more than one mother who, after the tests of 1962, scoured country stores for cans of milk with old serial numbers, dating from 1961, so that their children, at least, should be uncontaminated.

This fear of physical contamination was given its most popular expression in Rachel Carson's best seller, *Silent Spring*. This transferred the fear of dangerous foreign matter getting into one without one's knowledge from the politically tendentious atomic tests to the politically neutral overemployment of chemical herbicides and insecticides; true, the Department of Agriculture was inculpated to a certain extent, but attacking the Department of Agriculture does not bring one's loyalty into question; attacking the Pentagon or the Atomic Energy Commission would. Miss Carson's facts may all be indisputable; but the success of the book was due, I think, not merely to the author's skill of presentation, but also because the fears she wished to arouse corresponded to the vague apprehensions in the minds of many of her readers. In a way, it was comforting to know that the dreaded contamination might be physical, rather than immaterial and ideological.

For, of course, the greatest fear of contamination, felt by a significant minority of the population, is the fear of those alien notions and values which are given the blanket label of "communism." The "communism" which is feared by the members of the various more or less subversive, superpatriotic groups, their followers, and those whom they can intimidate, must be put within quotation marks; for, with insignificant exceptions, these ideas and attitudes have no visible connection with the ideology of communism in the U. S. S. R. or China, nor indeed with those of European or American Communist parties. It would seem to be an ethical, almost a religious dread, rather than a political attitude; the devil and his minions are abroad in the land, and will take possession of our souls, if we are not continuously vigilant. The professional anti-"communists" see themselves as the only alert guardians of a nation in peril.

Most of those intellectuals and liberals (in the American sense of the term) who lived through the years of Senator McCarthy's ascendancy, consider that the heyday of the superpatriots has passed, that they are no longer a significant component of the national scene; and indeed on the federal level this is clearly correct. They now have no national spokesman of even the coherence of the late Senator from Wisconsin nor one in an equivalent official position; the publicity available to the superpatriots is very much less.

Now that they are no longer personally threatened, as many of them felt themselves to be a decade ago, the liberals and intellectuals tend to ignore the superpatriots. One of the things which most surprised me on my return to the United States was the almost complete absence of communication between the two groups. Within the cities and larger towns, it seemed as though the only link between these two most vociferous sections of political opinion was the tenuous bond of kinship: "I don't know any myself, but my sister is married to a guy out in ———— who holds the most extreme opinions. No, we seldom meet; and never discuss politics."

In the suburbs and in the smaller towns the situation is very different. Even if social intercourse is kept down to the minimum, the superpatriots and the liberals are well aware of one another; and since the superpatriots tend to be well organized, often in clandestine conspiratorial groups, of which the John Birch society is at present the best known, they are able to exert an influence quite out of proportion to their numbers. In such local affairs as membership of school boards or the election to church elders or library committees, they practically exercise the right of veto; by putting about the charge that a potential candidate is a "communist" or "soft on communism," either by a whispering campaign or by leaflets, they seem to be able to frighten enough respectable voters to make it very hard for a man or woman so charged to be elected. The same type of negative power is influential in local and even to a considerable extent in state elections; but on the federal level, as far as I could judge, they have no such influence.

It is puzzling that this charge of "communism" should be so damaging and should frighten so many of the politically indifferent to the extent of influencing their votes. It can be leveled on the slenderest evidence, or even on no evidence at all; connection with or approval for such international organizations as the United Nations, or even support for the efforts of the administration to avoid war with Russia are the most frequent specific charges.

I would tend to connect this phobic fear of "communism" with the view of the personality implicit in the American naturalization laws and procedures. This view implies that adults can easily change their personalities and their allegiances, that they can be transformed from Europeans into Americans; and that, given the proper training, the children of the European-born can become hundred per cent Americans. But if adults and children can be transformed one way, they can be transformed another; and the uncanny phrase "brain-washing" suggests that this can be done against a person's will or consent, even, by extension, without his knowledge. The processes which built the American citizenry might, conceivably, be reversed; and since these frightened people ascribe diabolical skill and cunning to the "communists," any deviation from their own rigid views can be taken as a sign that this process is under way.

The invention of the phrase "brain-washing"—originally a literal translation from the Chinese—as a description of forcible conversion or indoctrination fitted the paranoid apprehensions of contamination which have been endemic among a minority of Americans throughout nearly the entire history of the United States and seemed to give these fears a "scientific" foundation. The "influencing machine" is a constantly recurring delusion among certain types of psychopaths; and here, it would seem, was the demonstration of the reality of such a concept. The careless journalistic use of the phrase to describe any type of indirect persuasion (perhaps particularly of advertising techniques) has kept the concept vivid.

I found it very difficult to meet superpatriots in a social situation; but of those that I did meet and talk to, a fair proportion seemed to me to show psychopathic characteristics. Apart from the belief that a great part of the administration was under the spell of the influencing machine, either unconsciously or, more usually, complicitly, there was the typical psychopathic incapacity to tolerate anxiety. The continuing confrontation of the ideology and military might of the U. S. A. and the U. S. S. R. (or, if you prefer, the Western world and the Communist bloc) is a situation fraught with anxiety for all aware people. The superpatriots would like to end this anxiety drastically, by atomic war; more than once I heard it stated that it would be worth sacrificing three quarters of the population of the United States if thereby the whole population of the Soviet Union could be destroyed. The people voicing such horrifying sentiments were not, and were not likely ever to be, in a position where they could have any influence on United States policy; but on the local level they were very busy, and did seem to have considerable negative power.

Since the superpatriots cannot influence the present administration, their hatred of it is rabid. Not even in the early days of the New Deal did I hear such malevolence voiced against "that man in the White House"; the President, his family, and nearly all the major figures in his administration are treated as traitors, as consciously furthering the surrender of the United States to the "communists." Any amount of evil-minded gossip is retailed as the "inside dope," as the "hidden truth." The existing government is seen as a vast conspiracy, which can only be countered by equally conspiratorial methods. To use a psychiatric metaphor, the country is seen by these superpatriots as dominated by "internal persecutors"; only the most violent and illegal means will save the America of their dreams from surrender to the "communists" or from demoralization by the extensions of this wicked government's sinister power—a process commonly referred to as "creeping socialism."

More or less clandestine organizations to protect Americanism from corruption by subversive and alien persons and influences (p. 196) have been a constant feature of the American scene from a very few years after the birth of the Republic; where the superpatriots differ from their numerous predecessors is in the location of the enemy, the source of corruption and contamination. Although the anti-Catholics suspected the Vatican of sinister intentions, and the isolationists the British Empire, the majority of the population never shared these unrealistic beliefs; up till 1945 the sources of contamination were essentially identified groups within the American population—Negroes, Jews, Catholics, the internationally-minded upper class of the Eastern seaboard, and so on. But today's superpatriots have identified the enemy in states which are in fact hostile and dangerous: Soviet Russia, Communist China, and their allies and associates. There is a far closer fit between their fears of hostility and evil intentions and the objective situation than there ever was in the past. The Communists *are* hostile to the United States and its interests, and *do* actively engage in sabotage, subversion, and spying. There is far less discrepancy between the delusions of the superpatriots and the views of the great majority of American citizens than there ever was in the past.

But the discrepancy is still there. The extreme violence and malevolence which the superpatriots attribute to the "communists" sound more like the projection of internal hatred and fear than any realistic appraisal of the situation. Following the classical psychological system of projection as a defense against unacceptable wishes, all the hostility is ascribed to the other, the enemy. It is, I think, significant that these superpatriots so constantly combine their accusations of disloyalty with accusations of homosexuality and ordinary criminal behavior; a "communist" is almost by definition a "sissy" or "panty-waist" and conversely; and criminals, especially violent criminals, are deemed either to be "communists" themselves or to be egged on by "communists." "Communists" are the repository of all the impulses which the superpatriots reject in themselves and fear in their neighbors.

Since they fear that "communists" will, as it were, effect a "de-naturalization" of American citizens, reversing the processes which have made Americans, the primary targets of their suspicions and accusations are those groups which have been most effective in turning immigrants and their children into Americans: teachers in the first place, the clergy, the people in mass communications, and, of course the government. The teachers above all (as could be suspected from the American scale of values) are subjected to the most minute supervision and the textbooks they use to the most ludicrous censorship; even the material used for teaching toddlers in nursery schools is suspect. In one case objections were raised to the source of supply of gramophone records for a nursery school; when the self-appointed censors were asked what was objectionable about the records used, they replied that the propaganda was "too subtle to be detected." In many California communities stores selling "anti-communist" and "Americanist" literature are erected as close as possible to the school entrance, so that the pupils may be decontaminated from any "communist" or internationalist teachings they may have received within the portals. As is well known, Richard

Nixon had as a major plank in his contest for Governor of California in 1962 keeping "communism" out of the schools; although he lost the election, the fact that so shrewd a politician should have thought it worth while campaigning against this bogey is a good indication of his assessment of the local climate of opinion.

The superpatriots are scared people; and they hope to achieve their aims by scaring everybody they disapprove of, from grocers selling Polish ham to politicians dubious about the prudence of invading Cuba or attacking Soviet Russia forthwith. They are not, of course, successful in their aims on the wider political scene; on the local level their influence is harder to compute. It seems to me very probable that they discourage the majority without strong political feelings from risking any statements or behavior which might give rise to persecution; they are one more influence making for the conformity and privatization of life in the small towns and suburbs which have been commented on by so many American authors and students of sociology. The safest life now is centered on the family, the local community, and one's business or profession; the pursuit of happiness has been given very domestic overtones.

The biggest superficial change in American life since I wrote The American People is the greatly decreased importance of dating behavior for adolescents and young adults. This has now been typically transformed into pre-adolescent behavior, suitable for youngsters in their earliest teens, the rehearsal for the social world of physiological maturity. Very shortly after this is attained, the prevailing pattern is "going steady," the boy and girl spending all their leisure time in one another's company, behaving as if they were betrothed; such practices as the "stag line" or "cutting in" at formal dances are said to be falling into desuetude. In this more concentrated relationship, the boy's aim is sexual intercourse, rather than the lesser intimacies of "heavy petting"; and, it would appear, he is frequently gratified, though the girl may retain some symbolic virginity (such as not undressing completely) until she is certain of marriage. Although some lip-service is paid to female chastity, especially among the church-going middle classes, there are no institutions left to help the girls protect themselves; indeed one of the reasons for young men attending a church of their selection is that this is one of the best situations in which to meet desirable girls. Outside the South, men are not responsible for watching over their womenfolk's chastity; brothers have no responsibility towards their sisters; and only a minority of parents will take the risk of having their daughter become unpopular and neglected by being more severe and circumspect than their neighbors.

A further hazard is raised by the fact that doctors and birth-control centers (in those states where they are not forbidden) conceive themselves to be guardians of morality, or fear to be accused of promoting immorality (if not of "communist" behavior) and therefore will not give advice nor fit appliances for girls who are neither betrothed nor married. Though this can be circumvented by purchasing a cheap wedding ring at any five-and-ten store before visiting the doctor, many girls, particularly those of the most admirable character, have a distaste for acting such a lie. Consequently early pregnancies and early marriages are becoming increasingly frequent; young people may be the parents of two or three children before they have completed their education. They will typically continue their university studies until they have got a B. A., for a college degree is being increasingly demanded for ever more unacademic jobs and positions; but with such domestic distractions and responsibilities it is unlikely that the academic work will be of much depth or originality. Intellectual adventurousness and early parenthood would seem to be mutually incompatible.

All the pressures on young Americans today make for domestic conformity: safety lies in early marriage (a full and normal sex-life), enough children, making the most of oneself both in appearance and in work, living in the best neighborhood one can afford and taking an adequate part in all the neighborhood activities including regular attendance at the church of one's choice, having a lot of convivial fun with one's neighbors and friends. Suburban (or, for the more prosperous, "exurban") life is now so developed that round nearly all the large cities are self-contained one-class communities. The city stores have felt it worthwhile to open a number of suburban branches; with what seems to be architectural perversity, they have mostly abandoned the convenient invention of a multiple store with different departments on different floors under a single roof in favor of what is dubbed a "shopping center" where all the departments are disguised as single shops, and it is necessary to go outdoors to get from one department to another. There is increasingly less reason for the respectable to leave their suburbs outside working hours, except for occasional "live" entertainment; the ubiquitous television seeks to insure that this want is felt by few.

Nearly everybody perforce travels between their suburbs and their place of work by private car; to accommodate these the most impressive and frightening speedways have been built all over the country. An eight-lane road with perhaps three levels of cross-overs is, from one point of view, a most impressive demonstration of civil engineering, on a scale and of a competence which Europe cannot approach; it is also a nightmarish, almost Kafka-esque landscape where man and nature are dwarfed to insignificance by steel and concrete. The daily, customarily solitary, drive in these inhuman wastelands must, one would think, convey a grim implacable message of man's insignificance.

A similar message is conveyed by the ever-increasing use of and reliance on electronic computers. Their speed and accuracy are, indeed, superhuman; and too many people seem to have adopted a variant of the nineteenth-century aristocrat's apothegm: "Live—our valets will do that for us." "Think—our computers will do that for us" seems to underlie the approach made by many scientists, whether they are studying the inorganic world or the behavior of human beings. The superiority of computers is very widely accepted, perhaps particularly by those who have only indirect understanding of the principles involved; in many cases one might say that the scientists are cowed by the "electronic brains" and tend to feel that, if a problem is not translatable into computer terms, then it is not a valid scientific problem. In an increasing number of American lives the human scale is being transcended.

An attempt to re-emphasize the human scale would seem to underlie much of contemporary American nonconformity, particularly among the young; to a very marked extent the pattern of contemporary American nonconformity is a negative version of contemporary conformity. Young men and women show their independence of mind, their rejection of the values of the "establishment," by not doing what their parents and their conforming brothers and sisters do: they refrain from making the best of their appearance, from dressing in the prevailing fashion, from living in surroundings of any elegance or owning any conspicuous durable consumer goods, in a great number of cases from smoking cigarettes or drinking liquor, from striving for success or promotion, from regular church-going, from any continuous or socially recognized family life; conspicuous disrespectability, intensity of feelings or emotions, and "spontaneousness" appear to be the chief values cultivated by today's individualists. Few generations in America's history can have been offered so barren an alternative.

The causes which earlier nonconformists were able to espouse are mostly no longer available. "Modern art," which over the last century the young were continuously able to advocate against their elders' vocal disapproval, is now completely and rather indiscriminately acceptable and accepted; few new office buildings are erected without some abstract mural or sculpture as part of the official furnishings or decoration. The obscene vocabulary is now so frequently printed or spoken, descriptions of sexual activity of every nature are now so commonplace in popular novels (all the magic has been taken out of the formerly taboo'd words and situations) that the young cannot any longer use any of the arts as a cause to defend against society's neglect or disapproval. Similarly, new scientific ideas are eagerly sought for by government, the universities, and the learned foundations; it seems unlikely that the early history of the psychoanalytic movement, or, for that matter, of radiology or relativity, have any chance of being repeated or that the advocates of a new science will again have to battle in poverty against general insult and incomprehension. That cause too has been taken over. Radical politics remain a possibility; but on the whole they appear irrelevant to most of today's nonconformist Americans, apart from the danger from superpatriots.

The one cause that does seem to excite the generous commitment of a sizable number of the nonconformist young is that of Negro rights, of racial equality. This cause, which is generous in itself, has the advantage of reducing all issues to black and white (in the most literal sense); the white demonstrators for Negro rights have the same certainty of being in the right, of sacrificing themselves for a just cause, as did their parents and grandparents when they demonstrated for the League of Nations against the merchants of death, for the right to form trade unions against the steel barons, for the Spanish Republicans against the fascists and pseudo-fascists in the U. S. government. This passionate involvement in the fortunes of others is a long-standing American tradition, dating from the earliest years of the Republic.

All such involvements have certain features in common. The passionate advocates divide the society into enemies and allies, the good and the bad, by a single criterion: what they say (far more than what they do) about this one topic. In all such cases there are identified enemies within the country; and anybody who does not condemn such enemies with the vehemence the advocates themselves use is suspect; they are probably secret sympathizers. It follows that the Administration is always on the enemy's side; for the Administration is the government of the whole country, and can never be as outspoken as the passionate advocates can wish. Even if, as in the present case, the Administration is clearly on the same side as the committed, it is treated as lukewarm, and therefore hostile.

Where this involvement appears to differ from the previous involvements of the generous-minded young in this century is in the probable time-span of devotion needed before its aims are realized. The earlier struggles were ended by success (in the case of the right to form trade unions), by defeat (for the Spanish Republicans), or by becoming irrelevant (for the merchants of death after the rise of Hitler); but the achievement of Negro equality demands a generation of family and social stability, of adequate education and training for the great majority of American Negroes after the disappearance of discrimination backed by law or by customs with the force of law. Even were all the injustices under which the Negroes suffer removed forthwith, they would still be the most disadvantaged section of the American population. Through no fault of their own, the majority of Negro adults are ill-educated, unskilled, frequently with understandably distorted characters; when potential equality is achieved, it will need a generation of attention and education before the potentiality can be realized, and skin color become truly irrelevant. In the meantime, the generous and public involvement of some young white Americans in the protests of their Negro fellow-citizens is more helpful to the respect that the United States wishes to command in the "uncommitted" world than any amount of material or military aid.

The attitude to the arts has undergone a major change since I wrote *The American People*. An interest in and appreciation of the arts is no longer considered effeminate, or sissy, or unworthy of a he-man. The enormous and highly publicized prices fetched by "modern" paintings is undoubtedly one component in their acceptance by hard-headed businessmen; another may well be the attacks made on abstract art by Mr. Khrushchev, on the general grounds that anything he opposes good Americans ought to support; but I would suspect that the major cause for rendering the arts respectable has been the proliferation of new architecture by distinguished architects for the office buildings of the most prosperous corporations, for new university buildings, new churches, new air-terminals, new embassies. Nowhere in the world, as far as I know, does the successful man spend so much of his time inside distinguished modern—not merely new—buildings.

These modern buildings tend to be aesthetic spectacles, the beauty of the façades and lobbies more important than the tiny humans who will live in them. The soaring concrete wings of some modern air-terminals are of the greatest external beauty; the furlong-long trek from the lobby to the point where one boards the plane is one of the most uncomfortable experiences, if one is burdened with young children or baggage, that travelers have known since the passing of the stagecoach. The glass-walled office skyscrapers soar into the clear air, transparent by day, an illuminated fairyland by night; the use of so much glass is, it would seem, in part determined by economy, to circumvent building regulations which fix the proportions of more conventional material; it is so impractical for a continental climate of temperature extremes that the buildings have to be hermetically sealed and air-conditioned. It seems as if such transparency has also a symbolic significance. It is a demonstration to all the world that nothing wrong, nothing subversive is going on inside this glass case, everything is quite literally open and above board; and, since the buildings are hermetically sealed, no unsuspected contamination can enter them. They are shining symbols of the soaring, aspiring, transparent integrity which Americans like to think—and not without justification—is their most praiseworthy characteristic. It is for the sake of integrity that the nonconformist young, living in the cheap city dwellings which have not yet been pulled down to make room for new office buildings, reject nearly everything that the glass business palaces symbolize.

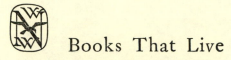

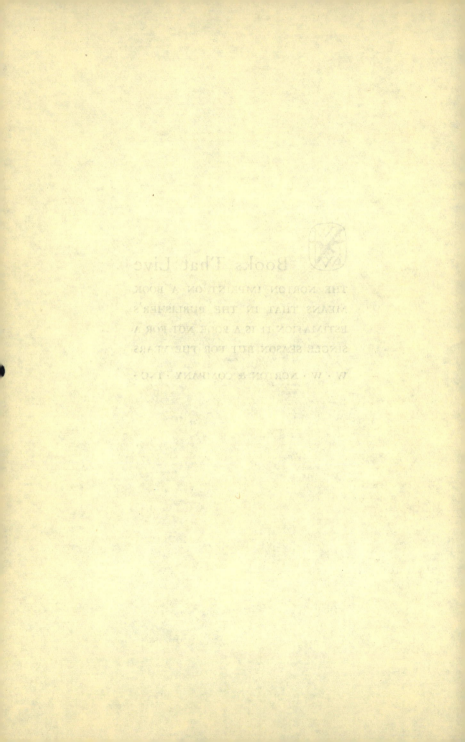

Norton Paperbacks on Psychiatry and Psychology

Abraham, Karl. *On Character and Libido Development, Six Essays, edited by Bertram D. Lewin, M.D.*

Adorno, T. W. et al. *The Authoritarian Personality.*

Alexander, Franz. *Fundamentals of Psychoanalysis.*

Alexander, Franz. *Psychosomatic Medicine.*

Cannon, Walter B. *The Wisdom of the Body.*

Erikson, Erik H. *Childhood and Society.*

Erikson, Erik H. *Gandhi's Truth.*

Erikson, Erik H. *Identity: Youth and Crisis.*

Erikson, Erik H. *Insight and Responsibility.*

Erikson, Erik H. *Young Man Luther.*

Ferenczi, Sandor. *Thalassa: A Theory of Genitality.*

Field, M. J. *Search for Security: An Ethno-Psychiatric Study of Rural Ghana.*

Freud, Sigmund. *An Autobiographical Study.*

Freud, Sigmund. *Civilization and its Discontents.*

Freud, Sigmund. *The Ego and the Id.*

Freud, Sigmund. *Jokes and Their Relation to the Unconscious.*

Freud, Sigmund. *Leonardo da Vinci and a Memory of His Childhood.*

Freud, Sigmund. *New Introductory Lectures on Psychoanalysis.*

Freud, Sigmund. *On Dreams.*

Freud, Sigmund. *On the History of the Psycho-Analytic Movement.*

Freud, Sigmund. *An Outline of Psycho-Analysis Rev. Ed.*

Freud, Sigmund. *The Problem of Anxiety.*

Freud, Sigmund. *The Psychopathology of Everyday Life.*

Freud, Sigmund. *The Question of Lay Analysis.*

Freud, Sigmund. *Totem and Taboo.*

Hinsie, Leland E. *The Person in the Body.*

Horney, Karen (Ed.) *Are You Considering Psychoanalysis?*

Horney, Karen. *New Ways in Psychoanalysis.*

Horney, Karen. *Neurosis and Human Growth.*

Horney, Karen. *The Neurotic Personality of Our Time.*

Horney, Karen. *Our Inner Conflicts.*

Horney, Karen. *Self-Analysis.*

Inhelder, Bärbel and Jean Piaget. *The Early Growth of Logic in the Child.*

James, William. *Talks to Teachers.*

Kasanin, J. S. *Language and Thought in Schizophrenia.*

Kelly, George A. *A Theory of Personality.*

Klein, Melanie and Joan Riviere. *Love, Hate and Reparation.*

Levy, David M. *Maternal Overprotection.*

Lifton, Robert Jay. *Thought Reform and the Psychology of Totalism.*

Piaget, Jean. *The Child's Conception of Number.*

Piaget, Jean. *The Origins of Intelligence in Children.*

Piaget, Jean. *Play, Dreams and Imitation in Childhood.*

Piaget, Jean and Bärbel Inhelder. *The Child's Conception of Space.*

Ruesch, Jurgen, M.D. and Gregory Bateson. *Communication: The Social Matrix of Psychiatry.*

Sullivan, Harry Stack. *Conceptions of Modern Psychiatry.*

Sullivan, Harry Stack. *The Interpersonal Theory of Psychiatry.*

Sullivan, Harry Stack. *The Psychiatric Interview.*

Watson, John B. *Behaviorism.*

Wheelis, Allen. *The Quest for Identity.*

Zilboorg, Gregory. *A History of Medical Psychology.*